CAMPAIGN 373

SYRIA AND LEBANON 1941

The Allied Fight against the Vichy French

DAVID SUTTON

ILLUSTRATED BY GRAHAM TURNER
Series editor Nikolai Bogdanovic

OSPREY PUBLISHING
Bloomsbury Publishing Plc
Kemp House, Chawley Park, Cumnor Hill, Oxford OX2 9PH, UK
29 Earlsfort Terrace, Dublin 2, Ireland
1385 Broadway, 5th Floor, New York, NY 10018, USA
E-mail: info@ospreypublishing.com
www.ospreypublishing.com

OSPREY is a trademark of Osprey Publishing Ltd

First published in Great Britain in 2022

A catalogue record for this book is available from the British Library.

ISBN: PB 9781472843845; eBook 9781472843852; ePDF 9781472843821;
XML 9781472843838

22 23 24 25 26   10 9 8 7 6 5 4 3 2 1

Maps by Bounford.com
3D BEVs by Paul Kime
Index by Mark Swift
Typeset by PDQ Digital Media Solutions, Bungay, UK
Printed and bound in India by Replika Press Private Ltd.

Artist's note

Readers may care to note that the original paintings from which the colour
plates in this book were prepared are available for private sale. All
reproduction copyright whatsoever is retained by the publishers. All
enquiries should be addressed to

Graham Turner, PO Box 568, Aylesbury, Bucks. HP17 8ZX UK
www.studio88.co.uk

The publishers regret that they can enter into no correspondence upon
this matter.

Osprey Publishing supports the Woodland Trust, the UK's leading woodland
conservation charity.

To find out more about our authors and books visit
www.ospreypublishing.com. Here you will find extracts, author
interviews, details of forthcoming events and the option to sign up for
our newsletter.

A note on measure

Measures are given in imperial in this volume. A simple conversion table is
provided below to help the reader.
1 inch = 2.54cm
1 foot = 0.3m
1 yard = 0.91m
1 mile = 1.6km
1 pound = 0.45kg
1 long ton = 1.01t

PREVIOUS PAGE
Troops of the 2/5th Battalion advance on the wireless mast at
Khalde. (Photo: George Silk, Australian War Memorial, 008595)

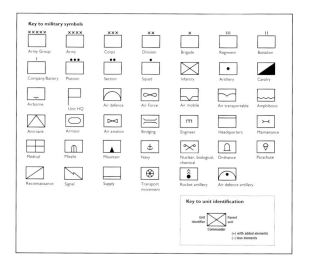

CONTENTS

ORIGINS OF THE CAMPAIGN

On 21 May 1941 General Sir Archibald Wavell pleaded with Winston Churchill not to be forced to open another front; 'you must trust my judgment in this matter,' he wrote, 'or relieve me of command'. The overstretched General Officer Commanding the Middle East already had his forces under attack in Greece, besieged at Tobruk, and fighting across North Africa, but Churchill insisted that he draw up plans to invade Syria and Lebanon – territories that had been governed by France since 1923, but since the fall of France had come under control of Marshal Pétain's government of Vichy France.

After its defeat by Germany in 1940 France was divided into two rough halves: the north of the country and its Atlantic coast came under direct German military occupation; the remaining southern half came under control of a new French government based in the city of Vichy that was technically neutral, but certainly swayed in favour of Germany during its brief existence. From 1940 to 1942 the Vichy government established an increasingly authoritarian regime, and was allowed to maintain military garrisons in its colonies in Africa, the Middle East and Indochina.

The Vichy occupation of Syria and Lebanon put the British in an awkward situation. Vichy France was in theory neutral, but the presence of an Axis-leaning force on the doorstep of British-held Iraq, Transjordan and Palestine never sat easy with policy-makers in London. Hostile powers in the region threatened British oil interests, and Syria and Lebanon were excellent territory from which Axis powers could launch attacks on the Suez Canal. From the fall of France onwards, Britain maintained that Vichy control of Syria and Lebanon would be tolerated, but that it would take 'appropriate action' against anything that might threaten Britain's interests: 'His Majesty's Government declare that they would not allow Syria or Lebanon to be occupied by any hostile power ... They therefore hold themselves free to take whatever measures they may ... consider necessary in their own interest'.

As the British looked uneasily at the French territory in the Levant, Charles de Gaulle – the leader of Free France – saw an opportunity. De Gaulle had refused to accept defeat to the Germans in 1940, and led the movement to fight alongside the British rather than choose the path of neutrality favoured by Pétain. De Gaulle had grand ambitions, but at the beginning of 1941 did not yet have a large army with which to realize them. In Syria and Lebanon he saw a chance. He was convinced that the troops stationed there – the *Armée du Levant* (Army of the Levant) – would defect from their Vichy

commanders and join the Free French in droves if only he could give them the opportunity to do so.

Into this volatile situation arose a catalyst that led the British to take the measures they felt necessary and the opportunity that de Gaulle needed to make them happen. In April 1941 Arab nationalist Rashid Ali al-Gaylani staged a coup in Iraq, overthrowing the pro-British government. The Germans supported the coup by sending supplies by air, which made their way to Iraqi territory via Vichy airfields in Syria and Lebanon. From 9 May, more than 100 German aircraft used the airfields on their way to support the anti-British revolt.

When German aircraft began strafing a small British force assembled in Palestine, the British became increasingly convinced that the Germans were on the brink of staging their own intervention in Syria and Lebanon. The British began bombing Vichy airfields on 14 May, and Churchill began seriously contemplating devoting already stretched Allied forces to a campaign to seize the region.

The bombing of Syrian air bases meant that the British and Vichy French were to all intents and purposes at war, and de Gaulle lobbied for hostilities to deepen. De Gaulle and General Georges Catroux, the commander of the small Free French force in Palestine, were convinced that if they were permitted to drive their small force towards Damascus, they would make short shrift of unenthusiastic Vichy forces, and that a swift victory would lead many of the *Armée du Levant* to rally to the Free French cause. De Gaulle stated that the campaign could be won by 'propaganda tactics and moral persuasion' more than anything else.

Catroux was vocal in his appeals to be allowed to attack, and moved his forces to the border of the Vichy territory in preparation. He told all who

Blenheims of Nos. 84 and 203 squadrons, RAF, based at H4 in Transjordan, attack Vichy positions at Palmyra. (Public Domain)

would listen that he had reliable intelligence – which turned out to be false – that Henri Dentz, Vichy Commander-in-Chief and High Commissioner of the Levant, was planning to withdraw the *Armée du Levant*, abandoning Syria and Lebanon to the Germans. Wavell, however, was unconvinced. Vichy officers in Syria and Lebanon, he argued, were generally well disposed to the British, but would certainly resist any encroachments by de Gaulle, whom they saw as no more than a traitor.

On 19 May Catroux held a secret meeting with Colonel Philibert Collet, commander of a Vichy cavalry unit, who disabused him of some of the more fantastic notions he had been spreading about the state of the *Armée du Levant*. Vichy forces were determined to oppose any invader, Axis or Allied, and were especially determined to oppose the hated Free French. Catroux sheepishly reported his findings to Wavell, who agreed that the Free French force was not large enough to take on the Vichy forces on its own.

This combination of lobbying by Free France, Germany's support of Rashid Ali's revolt, and persistent fears of wider German operations in the region led Churchill on 20 May to give the invasion of Syria and Lebanon the green light. A combined British and Free French force was to attack Vichy-held Syria and Lebanon, preventing the Germans from moving into the territory and possibly bringing new troops to the Free French cause. Wavell opposed the scheme, but eventually relented and drew up plans for the invasion – Operation *Exporter*.

CHRONOLOGY

1940

18 June   De Gaulle publically appeals to the French to resist German occupation.

22 June   France signs the armistice with Germany at Compiègne, it comes into effect on 25 June.

28 December   Henri Dentz arrives as new High Commissioner and Commander-in-Chief in the Levant.

1941

1 April   Rashid Ali stages anti-British coup in Iraq.

9 May   German aircraft begin using Vichy airfields in Syria and Lebanon to support Ali's coup.

14 May   British aircraft begin bombing Vichy airfields in Syria and Lebanon.

20 May   Churchill calls for invasion plan for Syria–Lebanon to be drawn up.

7–8 June   Operation *Exporter* begins.

9 June   Allied forces enter Khiam, Deraa, Sheikh Meskine, Kuneitra and Ezraa.

11 June   Allied troops enter Merdjayoun.

14 June   Allied forces enter Jezzine.

15 June   Allied forces enter Sidon; Vichy French launch major counter-attack.

16 June   1/Royal Fusiliers surrender at Kuneitra; *Le Chevalier Paul* sunk by Allied aircraft near Rouad Island.

18 June   Indian troops enter Mezze.

19 June   Vichy forces besiege Indian forces at Mezze.

20 June   Indian troops surrender at Mezze.

21 June   Allied forces enter Damascus.

24 June   Allied forces re-enter Merdjayoun; fighting begins to take the Jebel Mazar.

25 June   HMS *Parthian* sinks *Souffleur*.

4 July   *Saint-Didier* sunk by Allied aircraft in the Gulf of Adalia.

6–9 July   Battle of Damour.

12 July   Ceasefire comes into effect across Syria–Lebanon.

14 July   Armistice of Saint Jean d'Acre signed, bringing the Syria–Lebanon campaign to an end.

OPPOSING COMMANDERS

ALLIES

General Sir Archibald Wavell (1883–1950) was a decorated veteran of the Boer War and World War I who had lost his left eye at Ypres in 1915.[1] By 1941 he was Commander-in-Chief of British forces in the Middle East.

Wavell was opposed to the invasion of Syria and Lebanon on the grounds that his forces were stretched thin, but on Churchill's insistence drafted the attack plan. Wavell saw Syria–Lebanon as a distraction from more pressing concerns elsewhere, resulting, according to some, in him not devoting the resources necessary for a swift and decisive conclusion to the campaign.

General Sir Henry Maitland Wilson (1881–1964) was a decorated veteran of the Boer War and World War I who had spent the first years of World War II in command of British troops in Egypt, as military commander of Cyrenaica, and then in command of British forces in the Balkans. In this last position he was commended for his skilful command of the retreat from Greece and appointed to the role he would hold at the start of the Syria–Lebanon campaign: General Officer Commanding British Troops Palestine and Transjordan.

1   All ranks in this chapter are given as held at the beginning of the Syria–Lebanon campaign.

RIGHT
General Sir Archibald Wavell, Commander-in-Chief of British forces in the Middle East. (Corbis via Getty Images)

FAR RIGHT
General Sir Henry 'Jumbo' Maitland Wilson, July 1940. (Corbis via Getty Images)

Competent and well-liked by his troops, 'Jumbo' Wilson, as he was known, was responsible for pulling together Habforce to deal with Rashid Ali's Iraqi revolt. He then commanded Operation *Exporter* until newly promoted Lieutenant-General John Lavarack took over on 18 June. Wilson was a talented commander, but his attentions were divided in Syria and Lebanon, and he commanded the campaign from the luxurious King David Hotel in Jerusalem, 100 miles behind the front line.

Major-General John Lavarack (1885–1957), born in Queensland, Australia, was a professional soldier who served with distinction in Salonika and on the Western Front in World War I. Lavarack began World War II as a lieutenant-general, but accepted a demotion to take command of the newly raised 7th Australian Division in March 1940. Lavarack commanded this unit for the first ten days of Operation *Exporter*, until promoted to lieutenant-general and put in command of I (Australian) Corps, a role that saw him replace Wilson as commander of the campaign.

Lavarack was an intelligent commander who, according to one biographer, at times 'did not possess the most equable of temperaments', but at other times was 'a delightful character with a wide range of interests'. Lavarack frequently clashed with fellow officers, including Wavell, whom he frequently (and justifiably) accused of being (equally justifiably) focused on North Africa at the expense of the Syria–Lebanon campaign.

Major-General Paul Legentilhomme (1884–1975) was a professional soldier who after being captured in battle on 22 August 1914 spent the bulk of World War I as a prisoner of the Germans. In the interwar years he served across the French Empire, and by the outbreak of World War II was senior commander of French troops on the Somali coast.

In June 1940 Legentilhomme was one of several French officers to rally to de Gaulle's appeal, denounce France's armistice with Germany and announce his intention to continue the fight alongside the British Empire. For this he was relieved of his command and eventually stripped of French citizenship by the Vichy government. Unable to convince French Somaliland to join Free France, he joined de Gaulle in Britain in late October 1940.

In January 1941 he was promoted to major-general and took command of Free French forces in Sudan and Eritrea. There, he attempted once more to rally his former troops in Djibouti to the Free French cause, and from mid-April took command of the newly created *1ère Division Légère Française Libre* (1st Free French Light Division). Legentilhomme entered Syria with this unit on 8 June 1941.

VICHY

General Henri Dentz (1881–1945) was a battalion commander and later chief of staff of a division during World War I. In the interwar years he held several important posts, including head of Military Intelligence to the High Commissioner in Lebanon. An army corps commander at the outbreak of World War II, he was given the dubious honour of formally handing over Paris to the Germans at the Hôtel Crillon on 14 June 1940. Later that year he was appointed Commander-in-Chief and High Commissioner of the Levant by Pétain.

De Gaulle described Dentz as a 'very conformist general officer who was disposed to apply literally the orders given to him by Darlan'. Dentz saw service for Vichy as a way to protect France from further German encroachments – to break the armistice with Germany would put France in further danger. Colonel Groussard, his former chief of staff, described Dentz as 'capable of being a brilliant and capable deputy … [but] lacking the energy, boldness and initiative needed to be a commander-in-chief'. He may have lacked imagination, but as Henri de Wailly has pointed out, 'This intelligent and gentle officer, lacking energy, boldness and initiative, held his own so effectively against his British opponents that they had to treble the number of their troops after they attacked him'.

General Joseph de Verdilhac (1883–1963) commanded the *6e Division d'Infanterie Nord-Africaine* (6th North African Division) in the Battle of France. Before the war he had been classmate and friend of Legentilhomme at the military college at Saint-Cyr, but unlike his classmate he did not rally to the Free French cause at the fall of France in 1940. While Dentz may have lacked boldness and initiative, de Verdilhac was an effective commander who responded well to Allied attacks throughout the campaign.

OPPOSING FORCES

ALLIES

By 1 June 1941 the Allies were, in Churchill's words, 'strained to the limit' in the Mediterranean and North Africa. General Wavell's forces were under attack from Lieutenant-General Erwin Rommel's Afrika Korps in Libya, besieged at Tobruk and had been forced to evacuate Greece and Crete. Despite this, a sizeable force was scratched together for Operation *Exporter*, with the initial invasion containing some 35,000 ground troops supported by air and sea.

Australian, British and Indian units

The bulk of the initial invading force came from the 7th Australian Division, commanded by Major-General Lavarack. While the 18th Brigade was besieged at Tobruk, the two remaining brigades, the 21st and 25th, each contained three battalions containing at full strength roughly 850 officers and other ranks divided into four companies. To make up for the absent 18th Brigade, Lavarack was also given command of the severely depleted 2/3rd and 2/5th battalions of the 6th Australian Division, which were re-equipping in Palestine after evacuating from Greece. The 7th Division was the second to form in Australia after the outbreak of World War II. For having waited longer to enlist than their comrades in the 6th Division, they gained the pejorative moniker 'the deep thinkers'. Consisting entirely of volunteers, the men proved to be excellent soldiers in the Syria–Lebanon campaign.

The infantry battalions of the 7th Australian Division were accompanied by mechanized cavalry of the 6th and 9th Australian divisions (the 7th Division cavalry was in Cyprus and did not take part), the Cheshire Yeomanry, a squadron of the 1st Royal Dragoons and a composite cavalry regiment formed from elements of the Royal Scots Greys and the Staffordshire Yeomanry. The Australian cavalry

The Royal Scots Greys in Syria, June 1941. (Keystone-France/Gamma-Rapho via Getty Images)

British troops leap from a universal carrier in the ruins of Palmyra, 1941. (KEYSTONE-FRANCE/Gamma-Rapho via Getty Images)

regiments used lightly armoured universal carriers mounted with a Bren gun or Boys rifle, or Vickers Mk VI light tanks, equipped with a 0.5in. machine gun. Each regiment was made up of three squadrons containing about 20 vehicles. The Scots Greys and Staffordshire Yeomanry composite regiment was formed as each unit transitioned from being a horsed to motorized cavalry unit, and used wheeled vehicles (light trucks and armoured cars) to move troops around the winding Lebanese roads. The Cheshire Yeomanry remained one of the few British cavalry units still on horseback, and this allowed its troops to patrol difficult and mountainous country inaccessible to other cavalry units in the campaign.

The Australian elements of the invasion force were joined by three regiments of artillery (the 2/4th, 2/5th and 2/6th Field regiments, using 18- and 25-pdr field guns and 4.5in. howitzers) and the 2/2nd Anti-Tank Regiment (armed with Ordnance QF 2-pdrs and Solothurn anti-tank guns).

The Allied forces also contained more specialized units such as the 2/2nd Pioneer Battalion and the 2/3rd Machine-Gun Battalion. Pioneer battalions were armed engineers used to build and repair infrastructure such as roads and bridges, though at times in Operation *Exporter* – such as in the failed attempt to retake the fort at Merdjayoun on 17 June – they were used as a regular infantry battalion. Machine-gun battalions were well-armed, motorized infantry capable of providing extra support to regular infantry formations with 48 Vickers machine guns (12 per company). The 2/2nd Pioneer and 2/3rd Machine-Gun battalions rarely served as fully formed battalions during the campaign, and instead typically served as companies scattered amongst brigades as necessary.

The Allied forces were handicapped by a shortage of heavy tanks, signal equipment, transport and anti-aircraft weapons. Allied leaders, from Churchill to Wavell, did not want to jeopardize Operation *Battleaxe* – the attempt to lift the siege of Tobruk and recapture eastern Cyrenaica from Axis forces – for the sake of the invasion of Syria–Lebanon. This allocation of tanks to North Africa at the expense of Syria–Lebanon remained a particular source of grievance for the commanders of the campaign. After the war, Lavarack stated his firm belief that better equipment, particularly tanks, would have prevented hundreds of Australian casualties. Wavell admitted, during the campaign and after the war, that tanks would have been put to better use in the Levant rather than remaining in the Western Desert.

Australian reconnaissance AFVs in Syria, 11 June 1941. (Keystone-France\Gamma-Rapho via Getty Images)

The second-largest group of Allied troops formed for the initial invasion was the 5th Indian Brigade Group, commanded by Brigadier Wilfrid Lloyd. Indian army units were organized much like other British and Commonwealth forces in World War II: a division consisted of three brigades each containing three infantry battalions. Two of the battalions were typically Indian or Gurkha, the third British. Senior officers were drawn from the British Army.

The 5th Indian Brigade, comprising chiefly the 4th Battalion, 6th Rajputana Rifles (4/6 Rajputanas), 3rd Battalion, 1st Punjab Regiment (3/1 Punjabs) and the

Indian troops in the aftermath of the Battle of Keren, Eritrea, in April 1941. The 5th Indian Brigade played a major part in the battle and then formed one of the main attacking forces of Operation *Exporter*. (Mirrorpix via Getty Images)

1st Battalion, Royal Fusiliers (1/Royal Fusiliers), was an effective volunteer veteran force, fresh from fighting against the Italians at Sidi Barrani in Egypt, and Keren in Eritrea. The brigade group also contained the Transjordan Frontier Force – formed from one horsed and one mechanized regiment of local troops commanded by British officers – and artillery, anti-tank troops, anti-aircraft batteries, sappers and miners.

In its early phase Operation *Exporter* was also supported by 'the apples of Churchill's eye': a 500-strong Scottish Commando ('C' Battalion Layforce, named after Special Service Brigade commander Brigadier Robert Laycock) mostly consisting of troops from the Highland Light Infantry, but also containing sappers and gunners. Based in Cyprus before the campaign and as yet untested, this unit was commanded by 36-year-old Lieutenant-Colonel Richard Pedder, of Woolston, Hampshire.

As the campaign wore on, additional Allied units were brought in to help turn the tide against the unexpectedly stubborn Vichy French defence: Major-General John Evetts' untested 6th British Division; Major-General William Slim's 10th Indian Division, fresh from fighting along the Euphrates in the Anglo–Iraqi War; elements of the 17th and 20th Indian Infantry brigades (attached to the 10th Indian Division); and Habforce, a 2,000-strong formation assembled in May 1941 to assist beleaguered British forces in the fight against Rashid Ali's Iraqi revolt, especially at the besieged base at Habbaniya (from which the force took its name). The Iraqi revolt had largely petered out before the bulk of Habforce could be brought into action, and by June its troops were scattered across Iraq conducting garrison duties, ripe for deployment into Vichy French-held territory.

Free French

The Free French component of Operation *Exporter* was the *1ère Division Légère Française Libre* (1st Free French Light Division) commanded by Major-General Legentilhomme. The backbone of the Free French division was formed from 24 officers and 900 other ranks from the *13e Demi-Brigade de la Légion Étrangère* (13th Demi-Brigade of the Foreign Legion) who had joined de Gaulle's cause in June 1940. These experienced troops, veterans of campaigns in Norway and Eritrea, were formed into the *1er Bataillon*

Free French soldiers in Egypt, 1940. (Bettmann via Getty Images)

de la Légion Étrangère (1st Battalion of the Foreign Legion), and formed part of Lieutenant-Colonel Alfred Cazaud's *13e Brigade Mixte de Légion* (13th Mixed Legion Brigade). The other two battalions of this regiment were *Bataillon de Marche No. 1* (colonial troops from Gabon) and *Bataillon de Marche No. 2* (colonial troops from the modern-day Central African Republic).

The second Free French regiment was Lieutenant-Colonel René Génin's *1ère Brigade Coloniale* (1st Colonial Brigade), formed from the *1er Bataillon d'Infanterie de Marine* (1st Marine Infantry Battalion), *Bataillon de Marche No. 3* (colonial troops from Chad, and veterans of the Eritrean campaign), and *Bataillon de Marche No. 4* (colonial troops from Cameroon). The marine battalion formed in mid-1940 in Egypt from about 500 troops of *3e Bataillon, 24e Régiment d'Infanterie Coloniale* (3rd Battalion of the 24th Colonial Infantry Regiment) – some previously based in Cyprus, some in Syria – who refused to concede defeat to Germany and rallied to the Free French cause.

The rest of the force comprised the *1er Bataillon de Fusiliers Marins* (1st Battalion of Naval Fusiliers) – a combination of sailors and marines who had deserted from the French Navy at the fall of France; a squadron of spahis (colonial light cavalry); an artillery battery of four 75mm guns; a tank company of 12 Hotchkiss H-39 light infantry support tanks; and a 350-strong contingent of Circassian cavalry who had defected from the Vichy French *Groupement d'Escadrons Tcherkess* (Circassian Squadron Group).

Originally from the Caucasus region, the Circassians were an ethnic group displaced by Tsarist Russian forces in the 19th century who had established themselves as formidable warriors in the Middle East. The Circassian cavalry was commanded by the charismatic Colonel Philibert Collet, a veteran of World War I with a long history of service in the Levant who possessed longstanding Free French leanings. On 19 May 1941, while still serving with the Vichy French, he met in secret with Catroux to discuss the potential of an Allied invasion. When Dentz learned of the meeting and attempted to arrest Collet, Collet marched his force south to Palestine, where three of his squadrons chose to join him and defect, while the rest marched back to join the Vichy forces in Syria.

Spahis fighting for the Free French, October 1940. (© Imperial War Museum, E 775)

Naval forces

The Allied advance on land was supported by the Royal Navy's 15th Cruiser Squadron commanded by

Vice Admiral Edward King. At the beginning of the invasion this involved the cruisers HM Ships *Phoebe*, *Ajax*, and *Coventry*, the landing ship HMS *Glengyle*, and eight destroyers. The ships that made up the naval component of Operation *Exporter* changed throughout the campaign. In total, six cruisers, 16 destroyers, and the submarine HMS *Parthian* took part in operations off the Lebanese coast during the five-week campaign.

Circassian cavalry with their commander, Colonel Philibert Collet. (Public Domain)

Aviation

The main air component allocated to Operation *Exporter*, under command of South African-born Air Commodore Leslie Brown, Air Officer Commanding Palestine and Transjordan, at the start of the campaign consisted of light bombers (Bristol Blenheims), fighters (Hawker Hurricanes, Curtiss Tomahawks and Gloster Gladiators), reconnaissance aircraft (Westland Lysanders) and Fleet Air Arm aircraft (Fairey Swordfish) – 68 aircraft in total. The bulk of the fighters came from No. 80 Squadron RAF (Hurricane I) and No. 3 Squadron RAAF (rearming with Tomahawk IIb), though Tactical Reconnaissance Hurricanes were also used by No. 208 (army cooperation) Squadron RAF. The Gladiator biplane fighters, though outmoded by their monoplane counterparts, were still surprisingly effective aircraft in 1941. The Gladiators used in Operation *Exporter* flew in 'X' Flight, formed at Habbaniya in the aftermath of Rashid Ali's Iraqi revolt, and had previously served in nos. 33, 80 and 112 squadrons RAAF and No. 94 Squadron RAF. As the campaign progressed, the Allies supported this main air component with a dizzying array of aircraft – including Vickers Wellington bombers – from regular and composite units of the RAF, the RAAF and the Royal Navy Fleet Air Arm.

Members of No. 3 Squadron RAAF by one of their newly acquired Curtiss Tomahawks, 6 June 1941. (Photo: Damien Parer, Australian War Memorial, 008198)

ALLIED ORDER OF BATTLE

Commander-in-Chief Middle East Command: General Sir Archibald Wavell

General Officer Commanding Palestine and Transjordan: General Sir Henry Maitland Wilson

General Officer Commanding I Australian Corps: Lieutenant-General John Lavarack (from 18 June)

ALLIED LAND UNITS

7th Australian Division (Major-General John Lavarack until 18 June, then Major-General Arthur Allen)
Divisional troops:
> 6th Australian Division Cavalry
> 9th Australian Division Cavalry
> 2/4th Field Regiment
> 2/5th Field Regiment
> 2/6th Field Regiment
> 2/2nd Anti-Tank Regiment
> 2/3rd Infantry Battalion
> 2/5th Infantry Battalion
> 2/3rd Machine Gun Battalion
> 2/2nd Pioneer Battalion
> Cheshire Yeomanry
> Royal Scots Greys and Staffordshire Yeomanry (composite mechanized unit)
> One Squadron 1st Royal Dragoons
> 57th Light Anti-Aircraft Regiment
> C Battalion, Special Service Brigade (Scottish Commandos)

17th Australian Brigade (Brigadier Stanley Savige) (in campaign from 29 June)
> 2/3rd Infantry Battalion
> 2/5th Infantry Battalion
> 2/2nd Pioneer Battalion

21st Australian Infantry Brigade (Brigadier Jack Stevens)
> 2/14th Infantry Battalion
> 2/16th Infantry Battalion
> 2/27th Infantry Battalion

25th Australian Infantry Brigade (Brigadier Alfred Baxter-Cox until 22 June, then Brigadier Eric Plant until end of campaign)
> 2/25th Infantry Battalion
> 2/31st Infantry Battalion
> 2/33rd Infantry Battalion

6th British Division (Major-General John Evetts) (in campaign from 19 June)
16th British Infantry Brigade (Brigadier Cyril Lomax) (from 19 June)
> 2/King's Own Royal Regiment
> 2/Leicestershire Regiment
> 2/Queen's Royal Regiment

23rd British Infantry Brigade (Brigadier Alexander Galloway) (in campaign from 29 June)
> 1/Durham Light Infantry
> Czechoslovak 11th Infantry Battalion
> 4/Border Regiment

5th Indian Infantry Brigade Group (Brigadier Wilfrid Lloyd; Lieutenant-Colonel L.B. Jones of 4/6th Rajputana Rifles from 12 to 18 June)
> 1/Royal Fusiliers
> 3/1st Punjab Regiment
> 4/6th Rajputana Rifles
> 18th Field Company, Royal Bombay Sappers and Miners
> 1st Field Regiment, Royal Artillery
> 5th Indian Brigade Anti-Tank Company
> Transjordan Frontier Force
> One troop 171st Light Anti-Aircraft Battery
> 9th Australian Field Battery
> One troop 169th Light Anti-Aircraft Battery
> One troop 171st Light Anti-Aircraft Regiment

1ère Division Légère Française Libre (General Paul Legentilhomme)[2]
1ère Brigade Coloniale (Lieutenant-Colonel René Génin)
> *1er Bataillon d'Infanterie de Marine*
> *Bataillon de Marche No. 3*
> *Bataillon de Marche No. 4*

13e Brigade Mixte de Légion (Lieutenant-Colonel Alfred Cazaud)
> *1er Bataillon de Légion Étrangère*
> *Bataillon de Marche No. 1*
> *Bataillon de Marche No. 2*

1er Bataillon de Fusiliers Marins (Corvette Captain Robert Détroyat)
1ère Compagnie Autonome de Chars de Combat des Françaises Libres (Lieutenant Jean Volvey)
1er Groupe d'Escadrons de Spahis (Squadron Leader Paul Jourdier)
1er Régiment d'Artillerie Coloniale (Lieutenant Albert Chavanac)
Groupement d'Escadrons Tcherkess (Colonel Philibert Collet)

Habforce (Major-General John Clark) (from 21 June)
4th British Cavalry Brigade (Brigadier James Kingstone until 24 June, then Brigadier John Tiarks from 29 June) (Major Gooch in command from 24 to 29 June)
> Household Cavalry Regiment
> Warwickshire Yeomanry
> Royal Wiltshire Yeomanry
> 1/Essex Regiment
> Arab Legion Mechanized Regiment
> 237th Battery, Royal Artillery
> 2/1st Australian Anti-Tank Regiment (one battery)
> 169th Light Anti-Aircraft Battery

5th British Cavalry Brigade (Lieutenant-Colonel W.L. Wilson) (under command I Australian Corps from 22 June)
> North Somerset Yeomanry
> Queen's Own Yorkshire Dragoons

10th Indian Infantry Division (Major-General William Slim) (from 30 June)
21st Indian Brigade Group (Brigadier Charles Weld)
> 4/13th Frontier Force Rifles
> 2/4th Prince of Wales' Own Gurkha Rifles
> 2/10th Gurkha Rifles
> 157th Field Regiment, Royal Artillery
> 13th Duke of Connaught's Own Lancers
> 127th Fighter Squadron, RAF

25th Indian Infantry Brigade (Brigadier Ronald Mountain)
> 1/5th Mahratta Light Infantry
> 2/11th Sikh Regiment
> 3/9th Jat Regiment
> 2/8th Gurkha Rifles (detached from 20th Indian Infantry Brigade)

20th Indian Infantry Brigade (detached from 10th Indian Infantry Division) (Brigadier Donald Powell)
> 2/7th Gurkha Rifles
> 3/11th Sikh Regiment

17th Indian Infantry Brigade (detached from 8th Indian Infantry Regiment) (Brigadier Douglas Gracey)
> 1/12th Frontier Force Regiment
> 5/13th Frontier Force Rifles
> 32nd Field Regiment, Royal Artillery

ALLIED NAVAL FORCES

15th Cruiser Squadron (Vice Admiral Edward King)[3]
Cruisers:
> HMS *Ajax*

---

2   Cazaud's unit is often listed as being *1ère Brigade, 1ère Division Légère Française Libre* (1st Brigade, 1st Free French Light Division) and Génin's the *2e Brigade, 1ère Division Légère Française Libre* (2nd Brigade, 1st Free French Light Division), but this appears to be an error stemming from the fact that the troops from the *13e Brigade Mixte de Légion* were largely drawn from the *2e Brigade Française Libre*.

3   Not all ships were operating off the Lebanese coast at all times during the campaign.

HMS *Coventry*
HMNZS *Leander*
HMS *Naiad*
HMAS *Perth*
HMS *Phoebe*
Landing ship, infantry:
HMS *Glengyle*
Destroyers:
HMS *Decoy*
HMS *Griffin*
HMS *Hasty*
HMS *Havock*
HMS *Hotspur*
HMS *Ilex*
HMS *Isis*
HMS *Jackal*
HMS *Jaguar*
HMS *Janus*
HMS *Jervis*
HMS *Kandahar*
HMS *Kimberley*
HMS *Kingston*
HMAS *Nizam*
HMAS *Stuart*
Submarine:
HMS *Parthian*

ALLIED AIR UNITS

Units allocated to the invasion (Air Commodore Leslie Brown, Air Officer Commanding Palestine and Transjordan)
No. 11 Squadron RAF (12 Bristol Blenheim IV)
No. 80 Squadron RAF (14 Hawker Hurricane I)
No. 3 Squadron RAAF (12 Curtiss Tomahawk IIb)

No. 208 (Army co-operation) Squadron RAF ('A' and 'C' flights, ten Tactical Reconnaissance Hawker Hurricane I; 'B' Flight, three Westland Lysander II)
'X' Flight (formed on 6 June at Habbaniya from eight remaining Gloster Gladiators previously used in nos. 33, 80 and 112 squadrons RAAF, and 94 Squadron RAF)
No. 84 Squadron RAF (three Bristol Blenheim IV)
815 Squadron, Royal Navy Fleet Air Arm (six Fairey Swordfish)
Additional air units[4]
803 Squadron, Royal Navy Fleet Air Arm (six Fairey Fulmar I)
829 Squadron (six Fairey Albacore from 10 June)
No. 127 Squadron RAF (two long-range Hurricane; four Hurricane I; three Gloster Gladiator I; one Gloster Gladiator II; formation of this squadron begins 10 June)
No. 37 Squadron RAF (Vickers Wellington IC, from 18 June)
No. 38 Squadron RAF (Vickers Wellington IA and IC, from 18 June)
No. 70 Squadron RAF (Vickers Wellington IC, from 18 June)
No. 148 Squadron RAF (Vickers Wellington IC, from 18 June)
No. 260/450 Squadron RAF (composite squadron formed from 23 June formed from ground party of No. 450 Squadron RAAF and air party of No. 260 Squadron RAF) (six Hurricane I)
No. 33/806 Squadron (composite squadron formed from 23 June when six Hawker Hurricane I of No. 33 Squadron RAF attached to 806 Squadron, Royal Navy Fleet Air Arm) (six Hurricane I)
No. 45 Squadron RAF (12 Bristol Blenheim IV, from 23 June)
826 Squadron, Royal Navy Fleet Air Arm (five Fairey Albacore I) (from 28 June)
No. 203 Squadron RAF (six Bristol Blenheim IVF)

4   Prior to the official beginning of Operation *Exporter* on 8 June, other aircraft participated in bombing raids, including Beaufighters of nos. 252 and 272 squadrons RAF, and Marylands of No. 39 Squadron RAF. On 7 June two Bristol Bombays of No. 216 Squadron RAF dropped leaflets over Syria and Lebanon advising of the Allied intention to invade.

VICHY

In contrast to the units that cycled through the Allied command during the campaign, Vichy land forces remained relatively static as any attempts to resupply by air or sea were severely hampered by the enemy.

Vichy land forces can be divided into two main categories: regular French and colonial units; and *Troupes Spéciales*, local Lebanese and Syrian levies regularly described as 'of doubtful value'.

General Joseph de Verdilhac had at his disposal the *24e Régiment Mixte Colonial* (24th Mixed Colonial Regiment), a new unit consisting of three battalions of non-conscripted French troops of the *24e Régiment Mixte d'Infanterie Coloniale* (24th Mixed Colonial Infantry Regiment) with two garrisons of Senegalese troops; six battalions of Algerian infantry formed into two regiments – the *22e Régiment de Tirailleurs Algériens* (22nd Algerian Colonial Rifles Regiment) and the *29e Régiment de Tirailleurs Algériens* (29th Algerian Colonial Rifles Regiment); three battalions of the *16e Régiment de Tirailleurs Tunisiens* (16th Tunisian Colonial Rifles Regiment); three battalions of the *17e*

Vichy camel troops, 1941. (AirSeaLand Photos)

Régiment de Tirailleurs Sénégalais (17th Senegalese Colonial Rifles Regiment) and one battalion of the *1er Régiment de Tirailleurs Marocains* (1st Moroccan Colonial Rifles Regiment). A typical Vichy infantry battalion contained at full strength around 720 men.

Roughly 3,500 men organized into four battalions formed the *6e Régiment Étranger d'Infanterie* (6th Foreign Legion Regiment). These were the most professional troops in the Army of the Levant and were a considerable obstacle for the Allied invaders. Vichy officers employed them with care during the campaign, as during the fall of France in 1940 many were suspected of harbouring de Gaullist sympathies.

The 340 officers and 14,000 other ranks that made up the *Troupes Spéciales* were considered mostly unreliable, and were mainly kept on garrison duty. The Alouite, considered the best local troops, spent the majority of the campaign in the north for fear of a Turkish invasion. The Druze and Djeziriot cavalry were rightly suspected of having pro-British sympathies, and the Circassians, though loyal, suffered from poor morale following the desertion of Colonel Collet to the Free French cause.

The main striking force of the Army of the Levant was its two mechanized units, the *6e* and *7e Chasseurs d'Afrique* ('Hunters of Africa'), cavalry regiments formed in December 1940 from the shattered remnants of forces defeated by the Germans. Between them, they had 90 Renault R-35 light infantry tanks and an assortment of armoured cars. Designed to work with infantry attacks, R-35 tanks were slow, and lacked radio and range, making them completely unsuitable for hit-and-run attacks. Vichy forces also had around 50 Renault FT light tanks, outdated and unsuited to the campaign, which were mainly used to protect airfields and as mobile bunkers.

The assortment of armoured cars employed by the Vichy French was a Frankenstein's monster of available vehicles. In 1940 the French in Syria and Lebanon had an array of obsolete machines such as White armoured cars dating back to World War I, Panhard TOEs (*Théâtres d'Opérations Extérieures* – Overseas Theatre of Operations), and White-Laffly AMD armoured cars. Realizing their deficiencies, in early 1941 the Vichy command embarked on a programme of combining available stock with newly arrived American Dodge 5-ton trucks, by June 1941 creating 180 'new' machines. The main new types

A captured Vichy Potez 25TOE, in Syria. (Photo: John Jackson, Australian War Memorial, P12424.066)

produced were the Dodge-White – a Dodge chassis reinforced with armoured plates from the White and White-Laffly cars, armed with a 37mm gun and Reibel machine gun – and the AM Dodge (*Automitrailleuse* – Armoured Car – Dodge), a truck chassis with a cube-shaped armoured body, armed with a 37mm gun and a twin-mounted light machine gun. Thrown into the mix were a small number of *camions-canon de cavalerie* ('cavalry cannon trucks') – an armoured Dodge with a 75mm gun attached. By June 1941 the Vichy French in Syria and Lebanon had 79 AM Dodges, 19 Dodge-Whites, and eight *camions-canon de cavalerie* at their disposal.

Vichy mechanized units were closely supported by an elite and well-armed support squadron formed from troops of the *1er Régiment de Spahis Marocains* equipped with five specially made armoured cars armed with a twin-mounted 37mm gun, a light machine gun and an 81mm mortar capable of being fired from the vehicle's platform.

Vichy French naval assets in the region, under Admiral Pierre Gouton, commander of the Mediterranean Fleet, consisted of two destroyers, three submarines, five minesweepers and an oiler. This force, assisted by air assets, did at times harass British naval activities, but had little impact on the outcome of the campaign.

The Vichy French had a distinct advantage over the Allied attackers in the skies over Syria and Lebanon. In early June General Jean Jeannekyn, commander of the Vichy air forces in the Levant, had at his disposal 130 aircraft, roughly double the number available to the invading force. The sharp edge of this force included 43 fighters – 18 Morane-Saulnier M.S.406 and 25 Dewoitine D.520, both capable aircraft, but not a match for the Hurricanes and Tomahawks they would be pitted against. Joining these were 37 bombers – a mixture of American-built twin-engined Martin 167F bombers, Lioré et Olivier LeO 45 medium bombers, and obsolete Bloch MB.200 aircraft – and a variety of observation aircraft, mostly Potez 63.11 twin-engined aircraft and 25TOE biplanes. Much like the Allies, the Vichy air component received considerable reinforcement throughout the campaign, from both the Vichy air force and the *Aéronavale*, the French equivalent of the Fleet Air Arm. These were for the most part additional aircraft of the types already used by the Vichy French, but also included six Latécoère 298 torpedo-bombers, and three ageing Lioré et Olivier LeO H-257bis twin-engined biplanes.

In total, these inclusions boosted the number of Vichy French fighting and reconnaissance aircraft from 130 to 229 between 8 June and 12 July 1941.

VICHY ORDER OF BATTLE

High Commissioner and General Officer Commanding: General
     Henri Dentz
Commander-in-Chief, Ground Forces: General Joseph de Verdilhac

VICHY LAND UNITS

Légion Étrangère (Foreign Legion)
6e Régiment Étranger d'Infanterie (Colonel Jean-Luc Barré)
     1er Bataillon
     2e Bataillon
     3e Bataillon
     4e Bataillon

Regular French and colonial troops
22e Régiment de Tirailleurs Algériens (Colonel Aubry)
     1er Bataillon
     2e Bataillon
     3e Bataillon
29e Régiment de Tirailleurs Algériens
     1er Bataillon
     2e Bataillon
     3e Bataillon
1er Régiment de Tirailleurs Marocains
     5e Bataillon
17e Régiment de Tirailleurs Sénégalais (Colonel Horault)
     1er Bataillon
     2e Bataillon
     3e Bataillon
24e Régiment Mixte Colonial (Colonel François Georges-Picot)
     1er Bataillon
     2e Bataillon
     3e Bataillon
16e Régiment de Tirailleurs Tunisiens
     1er Bataillon
     2e Bataillon
     3e Bataillon

Troupes Spéciales (Special Troops)
Bataillons du Levant
     1er Bataillon
     2e Bataillon
     3e Bataillon
     4e Bataillon
     5e Bataillon
     6e Bataillon
     7e Bataillon
     8e Bataillon
Chasseurs Libanais
     1er Bataillon
     2e Bataillon
     3e Bataillon

Cavalry
6e Régiment de Chasseurs d'Afrique (Lieutenant-Colonel Charles
     Amanrich)
     1er escadron
     2e escadron
7e Régiment de Chasseurs d'Afrique (Lieutenant-Colonel Le Couteulx
     de Caumont)
     1er escadron
     2e escadron

Spahis
8e Régiment de Spahis Algériens
1er Régiment de Spahis Marocains
4e Régiment de Spahis Tunisiens
2e Régiment de Marche de Spahis

Cavalrie Spéciale (Special Cavalry)
33 companies (*Compagnie Légère du Désert* – Light Desert Company)
     formed from Druze, Djezireh, Tcherkess and Méhariste.

Artillery
Régiment d'Artillerie Coloniale du Levant
Régiment d'Artillerie Métropolitaine du Levant

VICHY NAVAL FORCES

Admiral Pierre Gouton
Destroyers:
Guépard
Valmy
Le Chevalier Paul
Vauquelin
Submarines:
Caïman
Marsouin
Souffleur
Minesweepers (five)
Cargo ships:
Saint-Didier
Oued-Yquem
Oiler:
Adour

VICHY AIR UNITS

General Jean Jeannekyn
As at 7 June 1941:
Groupe de Chasse I/7 (18 Morane-Saulnier M.S.406)
Groupe de Bombardement I/39 (12 Martin 167F)
Escadrille Bombardement 3/39 (six Bloch MB. 200) (training group
     formed in 1940 from within *Groupe de Bombardement I/39*)
Groupe de Reconnaissance II/39 (12 Potez 63-11) (reinforced with one
     Potez 63-11 on 8 July)
Groupe Aérien d'Observation 583 (five Potez 63-11) (reinforced with
     one Potez 63-11 on 8 July)
Escadrille d'Observation 592 (six Potez 25TOE)
Escadrille d'Observation 593 (six Potez 25TOE)
Escadrille d'Observation 594 (six Potez 25TOE)
Escadrille d'Observation 595 (six Potez 25TOE)
Escadrille d'Observation 596 (four Potez 25TOE)
Aéronavale Escadrille 19S (five Loire 130)
Groupe de Chasse III/6 (25 Dewoitine D.520 fighters) (reinforced with
     two D.520 on 4 July)
Groupe de Bombardement I/25 (ten Lioré et Olivier LeO 45) from
     14 June
Groupe de Bombardement I/31 (nine Lioré et Olivier LeO 45 from
     10 June)
Additional aircraft:
Groupe de Chasse II/3 (21 D.520) (arrives 15 June) (three D520 arrive
     as reinforcement 4 July)
Groupe de Chasse I/2 (ten D.520) (arrives 10 June)
Training school at Aulnot (four M.S.406 arrive 10 June)
Groupe de Bombardement I/12 (13 Lioré et Olivier 451) (joins *Groupe
     de Bombardement I/31* on 14 June)
Groupe de Reconnaissance I/22 (eight M167F) begin to arrive from
     21 June (reinforced by five M167F on 5 July)
Aéronavale Escadrille 6B, part of *Flotille 4F* (seven M167F) (arrives
     15 June)
Aéronavale Escadrille 7B, part of *Flotille 4F* (seven M167F) (arrives
     17 June)
Aéronavale Escadrille 1AC (12 D.520) (arrives 4 July)
Escadrille 1T (six Latécoère 298) (arrives 4 July)
Aéronavale Escadrille 1E (three Lioré et Olivier H-257bis) (arrives
     9 July)

OPPOSING PLANS

ALLIES

Once Churchill had decided to proceed with the invasion of Syria–Lebanon, the task of organizing the attack fell to Wavell who, despite his protestations, consulted with Wilson and drew up the invasion plan. Like every invasion plan of the region drawn up since antiquity, it was heavily dictated by geography. In the west, two parallel mountain ranges, the Lebanons and Anti-Lebanons, sliced by deep rivers and valleys, stretch from the Mediterranean coast to the border between Syria and Lebanon. In taking this mountainous country, it was necessary to follow established roads and direct artillery from key valleys and high points. In the east, the mountains give way to flat desert hemmed in on the south-east by the Jebel Druze, a vast, untamed hilly and rocky area impassable for tanks and other vehicles.

The plan for the Allied invasion of Syria–Lebanon, codenamed Operation *Exporter*, consisted of three main land thrusts north from British-controlled Palestine and Transjordan, supported by air and sea. On the left, the 21st Australian Brigade would advance along the coast to Beirut; in the centre, the 25th Australian Brigade would advance through the mountains and valleys of Lebanon to the rail hub and air base at Rayak; on the right the 5th Indian Brigade and Free French force would advance through the desert and seize Damascus. Once the first phase of the invasion was complete, the 21st Brigade would continue along the coast to Tripoli; the 25th Brigade to Homs; and the Indians and Free French to Palmyra. This three-pronged invasion plan took control of all major rail hubs, air bases and urban administrative centres in Vichy French-controlled Syria and Lebanon. The Tripoli–Homs–Palmyra line also secured the oil pipeline that ran from Iraq to the Mediterranean coast.

The land campaign would be supported by Allied air forces attacking enemy lines, aircraft, infrastructure and air bases. At sea, the Royal Navy would provide heavy fire for the coastal advance and implement a blockade to prevent Vichy reinforcements arriving by sea.

The plan for Operation *Exporter* has received fair criticism for its three-pronged approach. Major-General Lavarack criticized Wavell's insistence that the main thrust should take place along the coast towards Beirut, and instead argued that the push through the desert on the right had more chance of swift success. Others have criticized the approach altogether, and argued that a single powerful thrust along one of the main routes would have been sufficient. Anthony Mockler, for example, noted that it has been clear since

The Allied invasion plan

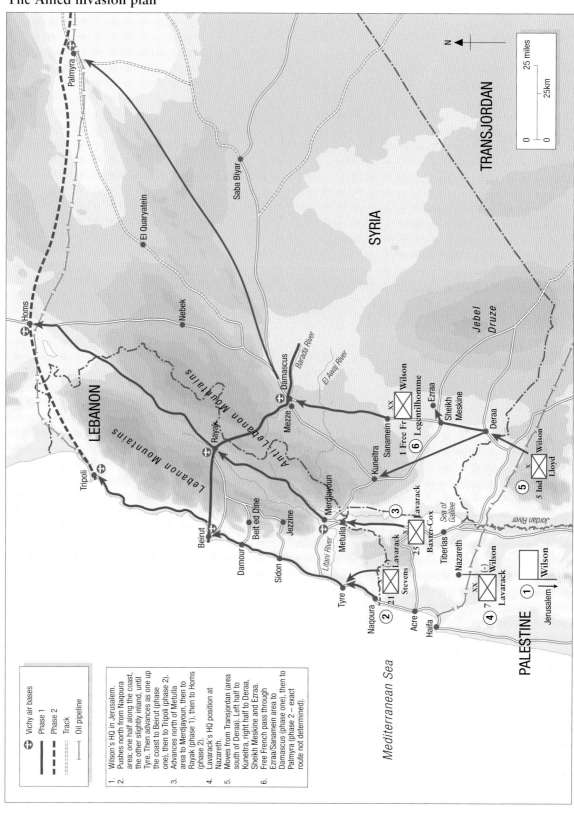

Legend:

- ⊕ Vichy air bases
- —— Phase 1
- ‐ ‐ ‐ Phase 2
- ········· Track
- ———— Oil pipeline

1. Wilson's HQ in Jerusalem.
2. Pushes north from Naqoura area; one half along the coast, the other slightly inland, until Tyre. Then advances as one up the coast to Beirut (phase one), then to Tripoli (phase 2).
3. Advances north of Metulla area to Merdjayoun, then to Rayak (phase 1), then to Homs (phase 2).
4. Lavarack's HQ position at Nazareth.
5. Moves from Transjordan (area south of Deraa). Left half to Kuneitra, right half to Deraa, Sheikh Meskine and Ezraa. Free French pass through Ezraa/Sanamein area to Damascus (phase one), then to Palmyra (phase 2 – exact route not determined).

Place names and labels visible on the map: TRANSJORDAN, SYRIA, LEBANON, PALESTINE, Mediterranean Sea, Jebel Druze, Lebanon Mountains, Anti-Lebanon Mountains, Palmyra, El Quaryatein, Saba Biyar, Homs, Nebek, Tripoli, Damascus, Mezze, Rayak, Barada River, El Awaj River, Beit ed Dine, Damour, Sidon, Jezzine, Beirut, Merdjayoun, Metulla, Litani River, Tyre, Naqoura, Acre, Haifa, Nazareth, Tiberias, Sea of Galilee, Kuneitra, Sanamein, Sheikh Meskine, Ezraa, Deraa, Jordan River, Jerusalem, Wilson, Lavarack, Baxter-Cox, Stevens, Lloyd, Legintilhomme, 1 Free Fr, 5 Ind, 7, 21, 25

ancient times that there are three main routes of attack from the south into Syria–Lebanon, and that by choosing to advance along all three, the British chose 'the most obvious, the easiest and possibly the least effective way to proceed'.

The flaw in the plan in part stemmed from the steadfast belief amongst the Allied command that the Vichy French would not put up a meaningful fight. Wavell and Wilson, believing de Gaulle's assertions that the Army of the Levant would defect to the Free French en masse, felt the approach sufficient to overcome a demoralized enemy. Believing that the campaign could be over in a matter of days, they ordered Allied units to advance with white flag and megaphone-wielding French-speaking officers to coax Vichy defenders to join their cause. Some Australian units were encouraged to march into battle in their distinctive slouch hats in the hope that the French might be reminded of the Australian role in World War I and thus be less inclined to fight. Within hours of the beginning of the campaign, as fire rained down on them, the Australians swapped their hats for tin helmets.

The coast road between Palestine and Tyre, *c.* June 1941. (Photo: Damien Parer, Australian War Memorial, 008759)

VICHY

The Vichy defence plan was similarly dictated by geography. Vichy French commanders knew that any attack from the south would come along one of the three main routes (or some combination of the three), and made their defence plans accordingly. The Vichy French knew their territory well, established defensive lines consisting of well-placed machine-gun posts and strongpoints, and ranged their artillery in preparation for an attack.

Syria–Lebanon was divided by the French into three military commands: North Syria, with headquarters at Aleppo and commanded by Colonel Rottier; South Syria, with headquarters at Damascus and commanded by General Delhomme; and Lebanon, with headquarters at Beirut and commanded by General Arlabosse. Vichy French Tunisian and Senegalese units were posted in the South Syria Command, the Algerians in Lebanon, and the rest of the forces, including the two mechanized regiments, kept in reserve. This plan was in part implemented because the defenders did not know where the emphasis of an invasion from the south would occur. If and when an attack came, the colonial Vichy French defenders could stall the advance before reserve troops were brought in.

Dentz's motivation to offer strong resistance stemmed from his conviction that he needed to defend French honour and neutrality at all costs. By Dentz's estimation, allowing an easy victory for the Allies in Syria and Lebanon would give the Germans cause to remove what freedoms Vichy France still enjoyed. When he first arrived at his new posting in Beirut in December 1940, he declared to the assembled officers: 'Get it into your head that what we are defending here is not Syria, it is French North Africa, because if we fail in our defensive mission, the Germans will take advantage of it to say: "You are incapable of using the weapons that we left you, we are going to look after French North Africa ourselves".'

THE CAMPAIGN

COASTAL COLUMN, 7–15 JUNE 1941

For the coastal advance on Beirut, Brigadier Jack Stevens' 21st Australian Brigade would attack in two columns. On the left, Lieutenant-Colonel Murray Moten's force, based on the 2/27th Battalion and designated 'Motcol', would advance with speed along the well-constructed road hugging the Mediterranean coast. Further inland, Lieutenant-Colonel Alex MacDonald's 'Doncol', based on the 2/16th Battalion, would protect the flank of the coastal advance in the foothills of the Lebanon ranges. Doncol would need to seize key Vichy border posts, take the winding road to Tibnine, and then approach Tyre from the east.

The remaining unit of the 21st Brigade, the 2/14th Battalion, along with the Cheshire Yeomanry, were under command of the brigade's headquarters. Parts of the 2/14th would be the first to cross the border closest to the coast before Motcol passed through. The Cheshire Yeomanry would operate further inland in the hills, protecting the flank of the advancing Australians, detachments of each being used as necessary in the initial phase of the invasion.

The invasion began on the evening of 7 June. Australian patrols, some aided by local guides, snuck into Vichy territory in rubber-soled shoes to cut telephone lines, overcome border guards and remove any charges on roads and bridges that they could find. The main body of troops crossed the border at 0200hrs on 8 June 1941.

During the first hours of the campaign the coastal column advanced steadily, though not as easily as expected. One mile from the coast at Labouna, a platoon of the 2/14th, after having been held up by the rough terrain, had to take the border post in a tough fight that included a bayonet charge. At 0700hrs, they heard a loud explosion: the French had blown up the main road south of Iskandaroun where it ran precipitously along a coastal cliff edge. The detonation created a crater 100ft long and 10ft deep. It could still be crossed by foot, but it would not be possible for vehicles to pass until 0500hrs on 9 June.

Further inland, the 2/16th Battalion crossed over from Palestine and took their border-post objectives while A Company of the 2/2nd Pioneer Battalion worked through the night to build a road linking El Malikiya in Palestine with Aitaroun in Lebanon. Once completed at 0400hrs, this allowed Allied vehicles (a squadron of the 6th Australian Division Cavalry and two troops of the 1st Royal Dragoons) to cross the border and advance further north.

The first day was a success: throughout 8 June Doncol units pushed forward, passed the former Ottoman castle at Tibnine and, after a series of skirmishes against retreating Algerian Spahis, entered Tyre without opposition at 1400hrs.

The next day, Allied forces massed in preparation for the major attack on the first main Vichy strongpoint that stood in their way – the heavily defended Litani River. The battle began in some confusion. As the 2/16th Battalion moved into position just before first light on the 9th, troops of C Company heard the unsettling sound of troops approaching at their rear. They soon realized that they had not been outflanked by enemy troops but were instead being approached by a group of Scottish commandos who had mistakenly landed south of the Litani and behind the advancing Australians.

The commandos had intended to make an amphibious landing north of the Litani on 8 June to prevent the French from destroying the stone bridge over the river and to sow confusion behind French lines. Their attack, split into three separate groups, was delayed by rough seas and when they made their landing in the early hours of 9 June, the operation proved a disaster. 'Force Z', commanded by Captain George More, made a safe landing two miles north of the Litani and within an hour had captured dozens of prisoners of war. They then became caught in a confusing fight in which prisoners escaped and attacked their captors. To make matters worse, French reinforcements arrived in armoured cars and they took friendly fire from the Australians to the south.

Lieutenant-Colonel Richard Pedder's 'Force Y' landed further south, but came under heavy fire as it landed. Pinned down on an exposed beach and seeking shelter in their landing crafts, when they attempted to push forward the reinforced Vichy French rained increasingly heavy fire on their positions. The commandos suffered 123 soldiers killed in action that morning.

Major Geoffrey Keyes' 'Force X' mistakenly (though perhaps luckily) landed south of the Litani, and assisted the Australians of the 2/16th Battalion in their fight to cross the river. Keyes would later become the posthumous recipient of a Victoria Cross for his actions in North Africa.

The 2/16th Battalion, working with the remnants of the commandos, faced a formidable task crossing the Litani. Near the coast the river, 100ft wide and flowing swiftly, was flanked by flat, exposed farmland. Further inland near a bend in the river, a series of ridges and ravines gave the defenders an excellent elevated position from which to pour fire on attackers below.

At first light on 9 June the 2/16th Battalion was waiting on the south side of the Litani when it received a series of rude shocks. First, news came that the only bridge in the area had been blown by the Vichy French. Then the Vichy defenders – *3e Bataillon, 22e Régiment de Tirailleurs Algériens* – opened fire. Machine-gun, mortar

The Litani River, 1941. The destruction of the stone bridge near this bend in the river forced Australians of the 2/16th Battalion and Scottish commandos to make a perilous crossing by canvas boat under heavy enemy fire. (Public Domain)

VICHY
1. I/8e Régiment de Spahis Algériens.
2. III/22e Régiment de Tirailleurs Algériens with artillery support.
3. Vichy French destroyers *Guépard* and *Valmy*.

DENTZ

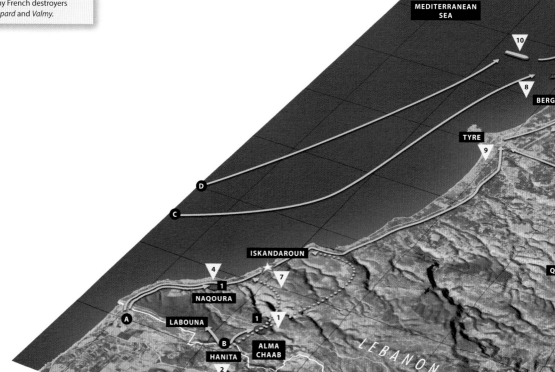

EVENTS

7 June

1. 2130hrs: Patrols from 2/14th Australian Infantry Battalion move out from Hanita, and set up roadblocks on coast road near Iskandaroun and north of Naqoura.

8 June

2. 0200hrs: Elements of 2/14th Australian Infantry Battalion move out from Hanita to attack Alma Chaab (D Company after a fight) and Labouna (B Company, without opposition).

3. 0200hrs: C and D companies, 2/16th Australian Infantry Battalion cross border and take Aitaroun (C Company, without opposition), Yaroun (D Company, without opposition) and Bennt Jbail (D Company, heavy fight after which 70 Algerian Spahis withdraw to the north). Their advance is preceded by a three-man patrol from C Company, which cuts telephone lines radiating from Bennt Jbail.

4. 0300hrs: 10 Platoon, 2/14th Australian Infantry Battalion attacks French border post at Naqoura. A platoon of 2/27th Australian Infantry Battalion, along with carriers, anti-tank guns and engineers, probes north of Naqoura and encounters a strong French party covering coast road.

5. 0400hrs: A Company, 2/2nd Pioneer Battalion completes construction of road allowing Allied troops to cross frontier from El Malikiya to Aitaroun (construction begins 0200hrs). Advance troops push north through Bennt Jbail towards Tibnine.

6. 0630hrs: Allied forces pass through Bennt Jbail and push north to Tibnine, where they engage in battle with retreating spahis. The spahis eventually withdraw in the direction of Nabatiyeh. An 80ft crater blown into the road and surrounding minefields delays the bulk of the units' progress until 1430hrs. Cheshire Yeomanry travels cross-country from Tibnine to Litani, covering right flank of Allied advance.

7. 0700hrs: Vichy French blow coast road on cliff south of Iskandaroun. The 2/14th Australian Infantry Battalion is able to pass through and press north to Tyre. Movement of vehicles delayed until 0500hrs 9 June.

8. 0800hrs: HMS *Kimberley*, after witnessing demolition of coast road south of Iskandaroun, bombards Vichy French positions north of the Litani River for one hour.

9. 1710hrs: Allied units converge on Tyre after it surrenders without opposition. Armoured cars of the Royal Dragoons and a patrol from the 6th Australian Division Cavalry proceed north from Tyre towards Litani River, but pull back after encountering heavy Vichy French fire.

9 June

10. 0450hrs: Scottish commandos make amphibious landing from HMS *Glengyle*. 'Force Z' lands near Kafr Badda and engages in confused fight in the hills north of the Litani River; 'Force Y' is virtually wiped out by strong Vichy French defences on the wide coastal plain; 'Force X' mistakenly lands south of the Litani River, and joins elements of the 2/16th Australian Infantry Battalion in attack on the Litani River.

11. 0530hrs: Australian troops, along with Scottish Commandos, begin attack on the Litani River.

12. During the Litani action the Vichy French destroyers *Guépard* and *Valmy* bombard the fragile Allied bridgehead north of the river before being driven off by 25-pdrs from the 2/4th Field Regiment.

COASTAL COLUMN, 7–9 JUNE 1941

The hard fighting encountered by Allied troops on 8 and 9 June on the coast proved that Operation *Exporter* was not going to be as easy as hoped. As Vichy French forces retreated north, they delayed the Allied advance through strategic demolitions and tough rear-guard actions. The Allied forces advancing inland were introduced to the mountainous terrain that dominated the campaign, and at the Litani River, the Allied attackers faced a fierce, determined and well-planned defensive position that made good use of the natural geography of the region.

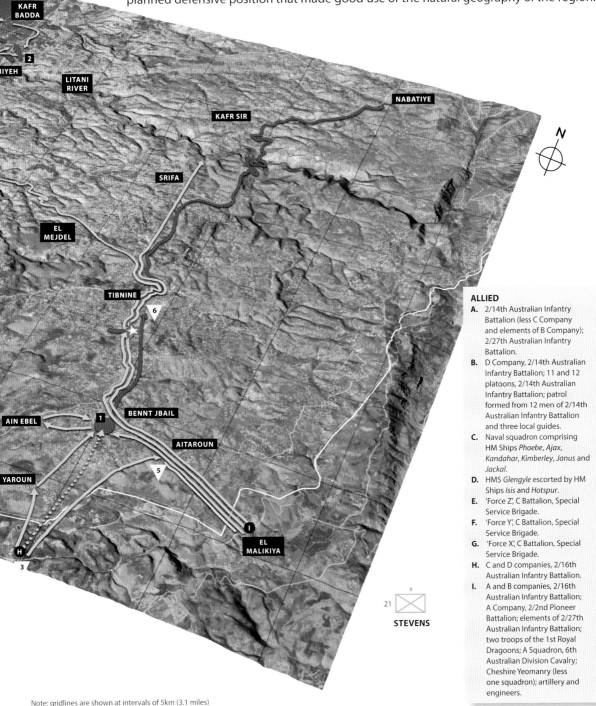

KAFR
BADDA

MIYEH

LITANI
RIVER

NABATIYE

KAFR SIR

SRIFA

EL
MEJDEL

TIBNINE

AIN EBEL

BENNT JBAIL

AITAROUN

YAROUN

EL
MALIKIYA

ALLIED
A. 2/14th Australian Infantry Battalion (less C Company and elements of B Company); 2/27th Australian Infantry Battalion.
B. D Company, 2/14th Australian Infantry Battalion; 11 and 12 platoons, 2/14th Australian Infantry Battalion; patrol formed from 12 men of 2/14th Australian Infantry Battalion and three local guides.
C. Naval squadron comprising HM Ships *Phoebe*, *Ajax*, *Kandahar*, *Kimberley*, *Janus* and *Jackal*.
D. HMS *Glengyle* escorted by HM Ships *Isis* and *Hotspur*.
E. 'Force Z', C Battalion, Special Service Brigade.
F. 'Force Y', C Battalion, Special Service Brigade.
G. 'Force X', C Battalion, Special Service Brigade.
H. C and D companies, 2/16th Australian Infantry Battalion.
I. A and B companies, 2/16th Australian Infantry Battalion; A Company, 2/2nd Pioneer Battalion; elements of 2/27th Australian Infantry Battalion; two troops of the 1st Royal Dragoons; A Squadron, 6th Australian Division Cavalry; Cheshire Yeomanry (less one squadron); artillery and engineers.

21 ⊠
STEVENS

Note: gridlines are shown at intervals of 5km (3.1 miles)

CROSSING THE LITANI RIVER (PP. 28–29)

The Australians were in a tight spot as they attempted to fight their way to the north side of the Litani River. Pinned down by heavy fire, the men of A Company, 2/16th Battalion sheltered as best they could in amongst the trees on the south side (**1**); 9 Platoon took shelter in a nearby graveyard and began to return fire (**2**). They could see that the river was running too strongly for it to be able to be safely paddled across in their canvas boats, so British-born Captain John Hearman, second-in-command of the company, decided to create an improvised pulley system made from painters (ropes) from the boats and cut telephone lines with which to pull the men across. Corporal Alan Haddy (**3**), a maltster from Perth who declared himself the best swimmer, then tied the ropes around himself and dived in. As he emerged mid-stream, he was struck and wounded by a mortar shell. He pressed on but began to visibly weaken, so Lance-Corporal Harry Dusting (**4**), a labourer from Woodanilling, jumped in to his aid. The two men got across the swollen river and tied the wire to a tree (**5**) to allow

their comrades to cross in their canvas boats in relative safety.

The first boat across (**6**) contained nine men from Kalgoorlie: Corporal Brian Walsh and privates Leonard O'Brien, Alphonsus Ryan, Alan 'Pud' Graffin, Robert 'Bobby' Wilson, Brian 'Blue' Maloney, Albert 'Chummy' Gray, Edmund 'Chook' Fowler and Frank Moretti. Each laden with all their gear and 300 rounds of ammunition, they crossed the river as mortar shells burst around them (**7**), then spread out to begin to form a bridgehead. As more men crossed the river an intense firefight ensued with heavy casualties on both sides. At one point the Allied positions came under fire from two French destroyers, *Guépard* and *Valmy*, until guns of the 2/4th Field Regiment returned fire and drew the Vichy French ships away. The daring crossing was forced on the Australians by the destruction of the Litani Bridge, but their acts allowed the Allies to continue the northward advance against strong and well-prepared defences.

and artillery fire was so heavy that members of the unit who had served in World War I described that barrage as being as intense as anything they encountered on the Western Front.

At the river mouth, the 2/16th Battalion's C Company and the commandos were pinned down and exposed on the beach. Although they could see enemy firing positions, they were unable to call in supporting artillery fire owing to a damaged wireless. In an increasingly desperate situation, the commandos and Australians used their one undamaged boat to get two loads of troops across the river under fire. Once across they were able to begin to scratch out a bridgehead on the north side. After capturing a redoubt that offered a commanding position over their sector, they slowly took control and were able to call in artillery support.

Further inland, the 2/16th Battalion companies designated to cross at the (now blown) bridge were in a dangerous position. They needed to cross at a bend in the river that was exposed to flanking fire from a ridge that towered over the river to their right. Caught in enfilading fire, some sought shelter in a nearby cemetery and attempted to return fire from behind gravestones.

Algerian defenders, supported by a battery of 75mm guns, had been in position on this natural obstacle since November 1940, plenty of time to prepare well-sited positions from which to lay down machine-gun and mortar fire and prepare extensive barbed-wire obstacles.

Once over the river, A, B and D companies of the 2/16th exploited the ridges to the north-east. A company of the rapidly advancing Australians, whose communications with headquarters had been cut, had to withdraw to the river to avoid coming under friendly fire from a planned artillery attack, and then further when mistakenly fired upon by HMS *Phoebe*. When the guns of the British ships fell silent and the barrage ended, they moved forward once more, reoccupying the ridge by 2300hrs.

By the early hours of 10 June engineers of the 2/6th Field Company, assisted by infantry, had constructed a temporary bridge over the Litani, allowing more men and vehicles to continue the northwards advance. On 11 June, when the Australians received reports that the Vichy French were warming up eight Renault R-35 tanks, Major Walter Rau of the 2/4th Field

The Javelin-class destroyer HMS *Janus* in 1939. (Public Domain)

Regiment, still in his pyjamas, led forward a 25-pdr and directed fire until the tanks withdrew. He then continued to provide supporting cover while under fire. Rau was later awarded a Distinguished Service Order for his exploits, believed to be the only DSO awarded to someone wearing their nightclothes. In the attack that followed, the Australians surrounded and captured nearly 50 Foreign Legion soldiers.

Vichy French forces of the *6e Régiment Étranger d'Infanterie* put up strong resistance at the Zaharani River, an important position that formed a natural obstacle on the northwards advance to Sidon, located at the beginning of the road linking the inland fort at Merdjayoun to the coast. After the 2/14th Battalion had made a series of disastrous attempts to cross the river, at 0615hrs on 12 June six Vichy Renault R-35s commanded by Commandant René Lehr – who had fought alongside the British at Dunkirk – crossed south over the river directly into Australian positions and caused severe casualties. A stalemate ensued; Australian anti-tank fire stopped the Vichy tanks from advancing further south but could not cause enough damage to force them to withdraw, and it was not until later in the day that troops of the 2/27th Battalion renewed the attack and were able to make a river crossing with artillery support.

Once across the Zaharani, Allied forces were poised to take the port city of Sidon. Sited on the Mediterranean coast and surrounded by a flat coastal plain covered in orchards and gardens, this was the largest city yet encountered by the Australians in the campaign. In an attempt to spare damage to its ancient mosque, Crusader-era castle and picturesque harbour, Brigadier Stevens hoped to take the city by diplomacy. He sent Lieutenant-Colonel Murray Moten of the 2/27th Battalion forward in the sidecar of a motorcycle with a white flag to parley. When Moten was fired on, it was clear that the French intended to put up a fight.

On the morning of 13 June the 2/16th Battalion launched an attack so disastrous that the date became known as 'Black Friday' to its troops. They advanced across exposed, flat country lined with high stone walls. The troops defending the area – the *22e Régiment de Tirailleurs Algériens*, elements of the *24e Régiment Mixte Colonial*, a company of Lebanese *Chasseurs*, three artillery batteries and three tanks of *6e Régiment de Chasseurs d'Afrique*, commanded by Colonel Aubry – were positioned along the northern bank of the Sataniq River just south of Sidon and in the hills on the right flank of the exposed coastal plain.

Although one of the attacking Australian companies was able to move along the far left to the north of the city, others were held up by stiff defence. By nightfall all companies of the 2/16th had pulled south of the town, where they spent an uncomfortable night seeking shelter in orchards or behind stone walls as Vichy French machine gunners swept the coastal plain. Early the following morning the

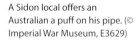

A Sidon local offers an Australian a puff on his pipe. (© Imperial War Museum, E3629)

Troops of the 2/27th Battalion advance along the Lebanese coast. (Photo: Frank Hurley, Australian War Memorial, 008250)

survivors pulled back to the south of the Sataniq to regroup. Seventeen men of the 2/16th Battalion were killed in action on 13 June, more would follow in the days to come.

The strong Vichy French defence offered at Sidon led Brigadier Stevens to bring the 2/27th Battalion into the fight. In the updated plan the 2/16th was to again attack along the coast towards Sidon while the 2/27th would attack in the hills further inland, concentrating its efforts on the village of Miyeoumiye about a mile to the south-east. Throughout 14 June, as the 2/27th moved into position, the 2/16th faced another French tank and infantry attack, which was seen off with the assistance of Allied artillery fire. When the two Australian battalions attacked on 15 June, they found Sidon abandoned. Lehr, seeing the large Allied force developing to his south and on his inland flank, had withdrawn north to Damour, 10 miles south of Beirut.

THE WAR IN THE AIR AND ON THE SEA

While the Syria–Lebanon campaign was largely fought on land, a vicious war also raged in the air and on the sea. Lavarack later wrote, 'Two factors of the highest importance which contributed to the British victory … [were] the bombardments provided in the coastal sector by the Royal Navy, and our superiority in the air'.

When Operation *Exporter* began, competing air forces supported ground troops, clashed over air bases (which lay at the core of the Allied invasion), attacked strategic targets such as ports, shipping and oil installations and provided air protection for naval assets. In the early hours of 8 June, Tomahawks of No. 3 Squadron RAAF attacked the airfield at Rayak, hitting six Vichy Morane fighters on the ground. During the battle for the Litani the next day, British fighters attacked Vichy twin-engined Bloch MB.200s as they attempted to bomb British ships, and French air ace Pierre Le Gloan added two Allied Hurricanes to his impressive list of wartime victories.

On the afternoon of 12 June Vichy Dewoitine fighters flew along the main coastal road strafing what they thought were enemy formations, mistakenly firing on a column of 100 Vichy prisoners captured by the 2/27th Battalion and killing ten of their own men in the process. When an Australian Bofors crew shot down one of the aircraft, it crashed into 2/27th positions, killing and wounding more men.

At sea, British and French ships clashed, supporting land operations on the coast and in the fight to ensure that Vichy French reinforcements did not arrive by sea. Allied ships supported the coastal advance by bombarding key Vichy French positions, some so close to the coast that the defending French could hear the sailors' 'hurrahs' as they hit their onshore targets.

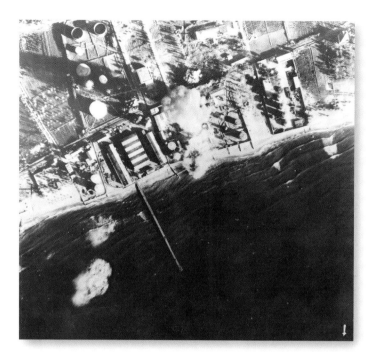

The Royal Dutch Shell oil depot near Beirut under attack by Blenheims of No. 11 Squadron RAF at the beginning of Operation *Exporter*. (© Imperial War Museum, HU93073)

Guépard and *Valmy* were driven off by Australian artillery fire from near the Litani on 9 June and were later spotted off the coast of Sidon by HM Ships *Janus*, *Hotspur*, *Jackal* and *Isis*. The French destroyers, which had the advantage of speed, lay heavy fire on *Janus*, which was far forward of the other ships, scoring three hits, including one on the bridge which killed 13. The disabled *Janus* was escorted away by the remaining British ships while the French destroyers sped to Beirut.

Flying officers Peter Turnbull (left) and Johnny Saunders of No. 3 Squadron RAAF, at Rosh Pinna, Palestine, 1941. Saunders was killed in action in the Middle East in November later that year; Turnbull in New Guinea in 1942. (Australian War Memorial, SUK 14924)

CENTRAL COLUMN, 7–15 JUNE 1941

Brigadier Alfred Baxter-Cox's 25th Australian Brigade began Operation *Exporter* by attacking in two columns, each aiming to push through the mountainous country north of Palestine, seizing forts at Khiam and Merdjayoun, and continuing north-east along the Bekaa Valley to Rayak, about 25 miles inland from Beirut. Lieutenant-Colonel Raymond Monaghan's 'Moncol' was to advance towards Hasbaya and Khiam, cutting the key road to Kuneitra further east along the way. To his left, Lieutenant-Colonel Selwyn Porter's 'Portcol' was to advance along the western edge of the valley to Merdjayoun before advancing towards the Damascus–Beirut highway to cut Vichy French movement between the cities.

Moncol and Portcol were to take Vichy French positions at Khirbe and Khiam, each a critical objective on the way to the key to the Bekaa Valley – Merdjayoun. Left of Portcol, B Squadron of the Cheshire Yeomanry was to advance on horseback to the main bridge over the Litani River (3 miles south-west of Merdjayoun), if possible establishing contact with the right flank of the 21st Brigade at Habbouch. The 2/5th Battalion and elements of the 2/5th Field Company were kept in reserve.

The central column's attack was preceded by a patrol ordered to cross the lines and disrupt Vichy attempts to sabotage infrastructure. For Portcol, the job fell to Sergeant Malcolm Davis, who was to lead eight men over the border shortly after midnight to prevent the bridge over the Litani River from being demolished and then wait for the arrival of the rest of the 2/31st Battalion by 0800hrs. After overcoming a small number of Vichy French sentries, the patrol could only wait as the bridge was blown and the battalion failed to arrive. The Vichy French had put up stronger resistance than anticipated and the main advance was slower than expected.

Moncol's main advance began at 0200hrs on 8 June. Captain Gordon Bennett's B Company, on the east of Moncol's advance, had been expected to reach its objective in the Hebbariye area in four hours. After becoming lost along the winding tracks, it took 24 hours; for the next five days it fought a series of running battles in the Ferdisse area. Exhausted and out of rations, Bennett's company silently withdrew through French positions and back to Australian lines on 12 June. The original battle plan was to meet up with the rest of the battalion on 10 June, but the Vichy offered stiffer resistance than expected, and their comrades were bogged down in a series of heavy fights near Khiam further to the south.

The fort at Khiam was a formidable obstacle, containing several machine-gun nests and surrounded by barbed-wire defences. During the attack on 8 June Captain George Connor charged forward, followed by five men, under artillery and small-arms fire, cut his way through barbed wire, climbed the wall into the compound and killed some of the defenders. The small party then came under fire from a machine-

Troops of the 2/25th Battalion in the mountainous country overlooking Vichy-held Lebanon. (Getty Images)

gun post on the opposite wall so took shelter and awaited support. Out of ammunition, they were soon joined by a French NCO and two medical staff who said they wanted to join the Free French cause, and five hours later had loosened enough stonework to climb out of the fort and back to the Australian lines. When Connor's company commander Captain Thomas Cotton then decided to attack through the hole created by Connor, his men came under heavy attack from the remaining French defenders, so the attack was postponed until the next morning.[5]

When the attack resumed on 9 June, the Australians found the fort abandoned and so moved on to Khiam village. The village was also abandoned, but the advancing troops were forced to stop when a Vichy artillery barrage ignited haystacks in the northern outskirts, creating an inferno that forced them to the south. From this point, the troops of Moncol consolidated their positions around Khiam, and the majority of the fighting shifted to Portcol on the left.

Portcol met stiffer resistance than expected as it fought through the steep and bare slopes of the Anti-Lebanon ranges. Allied planners of Operation *Exporter* had expected to move easily forwards and overcome Vichy defences in the dark of night. The main defences were so far north, however, that the advancing Allies did not reach the main defensive lines until daybreak; Vichy forces could see the advancing Australians and held their fire until at a close range.

At Khirbe a Free French liaison officer attached to the 2/31st Battalion was fired on as he approached Vichy defences with a white flag; the defenders would not be as easily persuaded to join de Gaulle as many had anticipated. When the Australians attacked the village, they faced extremely heavy fire from a series of well-positioned pillboxes and were forced to withdraw under artillery support.

As Portcol and Moncol attacked Khirbe and Khiam, B Squadron of the Cheshire Yeomanry took Blida after negotiating surrender from the Vichy

---

5   In 1944 Connor was awarded, rather puzzlingly, but in recognition of the shared victory of the Allies, the USSR Order of the
     Patriotic War (1st Class) by the Soviet government for his actions at Khiam three years before.

defenders. It then moved north to the Kafr Giladi area, where, mistaken for Vichy French spahis, it came under fire from Australian artillery.

At 1030hrs, Lieutenant-Colonel Porter renewed the attack on Khirbe, this time with three light tanks of the 6th Australian Cavalry in the lead. The tanks were able to destroy three machine-gun posts, but in doing so drew heavy French fire. Two were hit by anti-tank weapons while a third withdrew after driving forward to rescue survivors. When the final groups of Australians withdrew at dusk on 8 June, they had not advanced beyond their positions at first light.

The advance of the central column did not encounter eggshell resistance as expected. Colonel Tony Albord, commander of the Vichy French Merdjayoun sector had built up extensive defences. The 25th Australian Brigade's report noted that the 'enemy defences had been well planned ... Small cairns of stones were erected everywhere giving the enemy range marks', adding, 'the movement of two or three men would frequently bring down a concentration of mortar, machine-gun and even artillery fire'. The stiff and well-planned resistance met by the Australians on the first day of the invasion stalled Operation *Exporter* in the Merdjayoun sector. If the central column did not advance as planned, the attackers faced the potential creation of a large salient from which the Vichy French could attack the flanks of the coastal and eastern columns. In response, Major-General Lavarack reinforced the 25th Brigade with troops of the 2/25th Battalion, who had been held back as divisional reserve, to assist with the renewed offensive the following day.

On 9 and 10 June 1941 the advancing Allies consolidated gains and made probing advances on French positions, while the Algerian *tirailleur* defenders prepared for a renewed assault. Three companies of the newly arrived 2/25th Battalion moved north through the deep valleys running north from Khiam to the Ibeles Saki area (the fourth joined Portcol further west). From there, they could dominate the roads leading north from Merdjayoun and help prevent the arrival of Vichy reinforcements.

The crew of an Australian Vickers Light tank Mk VI at rest, 11 June 1941. (Australian War Memorial, 042209)

On 11 June the Allies renewed the offensive: the 2/31st Battalion, with considerable artillery support commanded by Brigadier Frank Berryman, attacked Khirbe and then Merdjayoun. On seeing the success of Berryman's artillery in the fight at Khiam, Lavarack decided that such firepower was the key to success in the area, and on 9 June he placed the 2/5th and 2/6th Field regiments under Berryman's command. The 2/31st Battalion would attack along the Khirbe ridge, and on reaching Khirbe its advance units would halt to take the objective and the rear companies would push forward to Merdjayoun.

The attack on Merdjayoun began at 0230hrs, 11 June, when the 40 guns of the 2/5th and 2/6th Field regiments opened fire along the Khirbe ridge. Each gun fired 130 rounds in a creeping barrage, infantry following closely behind the falling shells. Although at times caught in enemy barbed wire and heavy mortar fire, the 2/31st Battalion captured Khirbe and pressed on.

Phase two of the attack, planned to begin at 1300hrs, was similarly preceded by artillery fire, but when the advance troops of the 2/31st Battalion entered Merdjayoun, they found it abandoned. As was so often the case in the Syria–Lebanon campaign, attacking Allied troops went into battle only to find areas previously defended by Vichy troops now free of resistance. The Vichy French put up a fight, but withdrew to new defensive lines once the attack became overwhelming.

On 13 June troops in the Merdjayoun sector received Lavarack's orders to take advantage of their new gains and push north along a winding track through the hills. Lavarack aimed to leave a small defensive force at Merdjayoun, while the majority of the 25th Brigade made for Jezzine, an important hub 16 miles east of Sidon, a position from which the central column could support the coastal attack.

The trek for Jezzine began at 2100hrs on 13 June along dangerous roads meandering through complete darkness. Trucks from a British transport company carrying troops of the 2/31st Battalion became bogged down in mountain streams and had to make three-point turns to get around hairpins in the road; one of the trucks overturned. Mechanized cavalry from the Cheshire Yeomanry and 9th Australian Division were especially slow. At one point they were forced to push a vehicle over the side of the road to allow others to pass. The 2/25th Battalion was held up and remained at Jerme. The Cheshire Yeomanry reached Mazraat Koufra but did not get as far as its intended objective at Zhalta. The 2/31st Battalion did not reach Kfar Houn, near Jezzine, until daybreak on 14 June.

The 2/25th Battalion having been held up, the task of taking Jezzine fell to the 2/31st Battalion, who launched their attack at 1800hrs on 14 June. The infantry, who had not had food or sleep for 24 hours, clambered down a series of terraced hills covered in trees and vines under enemy fire, crossed 100 yards of flat country well covered by fixed Vichy machine-gun positions, climbed up a steep hill overlooking Jezzine, and then down a steep, terraced and vine-covered slope into the town. During the attack New Zealand-born Private Samuel Luff, on seeing a company on his left pinned down by machine-gun fire, snuck to the rear of the French position and killed all five defenders with his rifle and bayonet. Luff would be killed less than a month after this action, on 12 July, the same day that the ceasefire that brought an end to the campaign came into effect.

When the battalion entered the town at 2030hrs, it was free of Vichy defenders. One-and-a-half companies of infantry and two squadrons of cavalry had been killed in the fighting or retreated. After the campaign Dentz told Lavarack that he had intended to strengthen the defending force at Jezzine on 15 June, a day too late.

RIGHT COLUMN, 7–15 JUNE 1941

The 5th Indian Brigade Group was divided into four columns for its advance into Syria: Lieutenant-Colonel Lionel Jones' 4/6th Rajputana Rifles, designated 'A' Column, was to press north-west from Mafraq and move to encircle the road hub at Deraa from the north-west. Brigadier Lloyd's 'B' Column, based around the 3/1st Punjab Regiment, would move from Irbid to encircle Deraa from the south-west. Once 'A' and 'B' columns had joined their pincers at Deraa, 'A' Column would press north and seize Sheikh Meskine and Ezraa. 'C' Column, based on C Company, 1st Battalion, Royal Fusiliers (1/Royal Fusiliers), was to move from south of the Sea of Galilee to attack Fiq. Lieutenant-Colonel Arthur Orr's 'D' Column, based on 1/Royal Fusiliers (less C Company), was to move along the western edge of the Sea of Galilee to attack Kuneitra. By taking Deraa, Sheikh Meskine, Ezraa and Kuneitra, the 5th Indian Brigade would set the scene for General Legentilhomme's Free French to pass through and cross the deserts towards Damascus.

In the final hours of 7 June the main advance of the right column of Operation *Exporter* was preceded by an advance party of infantry, sappers and miners drawn from 'A' Column, with a Free French guide, which crossed the border and secured key posts and infrastructure such as the viaduct and bridge at Tell Chebab. The bulk of the 5th Indian Brigade began its advance at 0200hrs on 8 June and made good progress throughout the morning. 'B' Column neared its first major objective, Deraa, around 0500hrs. After a car sent forward to parley was fired on, the 3/1st Punjabs waited for the arrival of 'A' Column from the north-west and prepared to make an attack. 'A' Column made good progress, and after overcoming light Vichy resistance its advance companies were ready to advance on Deraa at 0700hrs.

The attack on Deraa began with artillery support, and within an hour and a half the three attacking companies of the 3/1st Punjab had entered the town and taken 250 prisoners. The 4/6th Rajputanas, poised to prevent any Vichy troops from escaping to the north towards Damascus, stopped some transports, tractors and lorries, but failed to stop a train.

With Deraa now in Allied hands, the Rajputanas began their advance on Sheikh Meskine, a small town 18 miles north defended by troops of the *17e Régiment de Tirailleurs Sénégalais* and a platoon of armoured cars. As they moved north, they faced sporadic fire from Vichy armoured cars and aircraft which dive-bombed and strafed the Indian lines of advance. The armoured cars were seen off by anti-tank gun fire. An Indian soldier fired on an attacking aircraft from less than 100ft with a Tommy gun. The aircraft was seen retreating with smoke pouring from its tail, though available sources do not shed light on its fate. Despite the attacks on land and in the air, the column pushed forward with speed and by early afternoon of 8 June was on the outskirts of Sheikh Meskine, planning its next attack.

Lieutenant-Colonel Jones' plan was for the infantry to advance on the west of the town with artillery support and exploit any successes. The attack began at 1500hrs but came to a halt in the face of strong Vichy defences. Amid heavy machine-gun and 75mm artillery fire, Indian attackers also had to contend with an intense blaze caused when dry cereal crops, prolific in the area, were set on fire by the defending French. Vichy aircraft concentrated their attacks on the supporting Allied artillery.

With the attack held up, Jones changed the plan and ordered his troops to swing to the north-west and capture a ridge overlooking the town. The Indians once more came under intense machine-gun fire, but pushed forward, overcame machine-gun posts, and then began to consolidate their position on top of the ridge as night set in. The push to the ridge, made under intense fire, was successful in large part due to the actions of Naik Bhopal Singh, commander of the reserve platoon of D Company, who single-handedly stormed the forward machine-gun post, killed or wounded the three Vichy French defenders and then attacked a second post on his right. Seeing his example, other platoons in the attack began to follow suit, attacked the other posts and pressed to the top of the ridge.

The Indians resumed their attack at dawn on 9 June, but as the 4/6th Rajputanas entered the town, they encountered no opposition. The Vichy defenders, having put up initial defence, had abandoned the town during the night. In taking Sheikh Meskine the Indian forces lost nine killed and 36 wounded and missing. The Vichy defenders lost 89 killed, wounded or captured, as well as considerable amounts of guns and other materiel.

On 8 June the Royal Fusiliers advanced on Kuneitra and sent a party forward to parley with the Vichy defenders – troops of the *17e Régiment de Tirailleurs Sénégalais*. The Vichy French agreed to a temporary truce to allow civilians to leave the town, but it was soon apparent that the defenders were stalling for time, so the British also used the delay to reinforce. During the truce, planned to last until midday, a Free French liaison officer was fired on. Although the shot missed, hostilities began in earnest shortly after lunchtime. The Royal Fusiliers met stiff defence and could not take the town, and it was not until the next day the Fusiliers found the town abandoned. An Australian artillery officer described the events at Kuneitra as 'mostly in the nature of a Gilbert and Sullivan opera because of the parleys, the envoys, and the flags of truce going to and fro'.

The first two days of the campaign had been a success for the 5th Indian Brigade Group, which had successfully captured Deraa, Sheikh Meskine, Kuneitra and Ezraa (entered without opposition by a company of the 4/6th Rajputanas on the morning of 9 June). The defending Vichy troops had also, for the most part, successfully carried out their duty. Where possible they defended their positions, and after having delayed the Allies as long as possible, withdrew to new defensive lines closer to Damascus.

The 5th Indian Brigade Group's successful operation allowed for General Legentilhomme's Free French force to begin its thrust towards Damascus. The Free French force, accompanied by a battery of the 1st Field Regiment, Royal Artillery and a troop of light anti-aircraft, passed through the Indian lines at Sheikh Meskine on the morning of 9 June. Their first main objective was the strong Vichy defensive line that ran along the El Awaj River from Deir Khabie to Kiswe, 8 miles south of Damascus, and then along the Jebel Maani, a ridge running south-east of Kiswe to Deir Ali. General Delhomme, commander of the South Syria sector, had selected Kiswe as the main area for defence on the way to Damascus. Aided by the natural defences offered by the El Awaj River and surrounding hills, the town was occupied by three battalions of *tirailleurs*: the *5e Bataillon, 1er Régiment de Tirailleurs Marocains*; *1er Bataillon, 17e Régiment de Tirailleurs Sénégalais*; *3e Bataillon, 29e Régiment de Tirailleurs Algériens*.

A member of the 5th Indian Division directs traffic on the Deraa–Damascus highway, June 1941. (Public Domain)

By the end of 9 June the advance Free French troops had reached Ghabagheb and Taibe, and captured Khan Denoun and Deir Ali. On 11 June, after a day's pause to reinforce, Legentilhomme ordered his troops to begin the attack on Kiswe: *Bataillon de Marche No. 1* to attack along the Jebel Maani, and *Bataillon de Marche No. 2* to push north in the rocky hills further east. The former met stiff resistance while advancing in the stifling heat on the Jebel Maani, but their countrymen to the east did not face any opposition, occupied the Jebel Badrane and pushed north to Al Horjelah on the El Awaj River east of Kiswe. They renewed their attack on the 12th, captured the heights of the Jebel Maani, but were unable to take Kiswe itself.

As the Free French advanced, the 4/6th Rajputanas, the 3/1st Punjabs and the Royal Fusiliers guarded their left flank, and *Groupment Collet* (Colonel Collet's Circassians) passed through Sheikh Meskine to protect their east. On 11 June Collet's force came under attack from Vichy tanks and armoured cars on the Free French eastern flank, but successfully saw them off with well-directed fire from their single 25mm anti-tank gun.

Overall, 12 June proved to be an eventful day for the eastern column of Operation *Exporter*. At the same time that mistaken reports of the Vichy French attack in the east came through, General Wilson placed the 5th Indian Brigade under General Legentilhomme's command so that the united force could renew the attack towards Damascus. That same day, however,

Legentilhomme was severely wounded in his left arm during a Vichy French bombing raid on his headquarters at Sanamein. Legentilhomme's wounding and the transfer of command caused a reshuffle of units in the area. Desperate to continue his command, he insisted that he could direct battle from hospital in Deraa until reluctantly persuaded by Lloyd to transfer the force to his command on 14 June. It was a depressing blow for Legentilhomme, who had taken enormous pride in the faith placed in him by the British in letting him take command of some of their units. Brigadier Lloyd took overall command of a combined force comprising the 5th Indian Brigade – recently bolstered by a squadron of armoured cars from the Royal Dragoons – and Free French troops. This new formation was called 'Gentforce'; Lieutenant-Colonel Jones of the 4/6th Rajputana Rifles took command of the 5th Indian Brigade.

On 15 June this reorganized force launched a major attack south of Damascus. First, the 5th Indian Brigade and Free French *1er Bataillon d'Infanterie de Marine* was to secure the Kiswe–Moukelbe area with artillery support. Second, artillery in the area was to pass over to the Free French, who would move through the Kiswe area and secure Jebel Abou Atriz and Jebel Kelb, 2 miles to the north-east. As the Free French attacked north of Kiswe, Colonel Collet's Circassians were to push north of the operation to cut Vichy communications with Damascus. The operation was supported by Allied aircraft bombing and strafing attacks on key Vichy French positions.

The Vichy defenders – three infantry battalions, a Moroccan spahi regiment, some Circassian units of uncertain morale and artillery – had a considerable task in the face of the much larger Indian and Free French attacking force. The Vichy defenders did have strong defensive positions along the El Awaj River astride the Deraa–Damascus road, and good shelter in the houses and gardens along the road, which was flanked by steep and boulder-strewn hills on each side. Allied vehicle movement was required to be made along the road, and the Vichy had time to prepare to meet that threat.

The attack, which began in the early hours of 15 June, initially went according to plan for the Allies. The 3/1st Punjabs found the bridge over the muddy El Awaj River blown, but were able to cross and create a bridgehead with the aid of 30 wooden ladders made by the 18th Field Company Sappers and Miners the previous night. Several hours of close-quarter fighting in the houses and gardens of Kiswe followed, but the town was captured by 0830hrs. After overcoming heavy machine-gun fire on their flank, the 4/6th Rajputanas passed through and took a series of small hills north of the village. The success north of Kiswe village was, however, short-lived. A counter-attack by fleeing troops scrambled together by determined Vichy officers forced the Indians to withdraw to the village.

Small-scale Vichy counter-attacks did not, however, prevent the second phase of the operation from commencing at 1100hrs. Colonel Casseau's African troops of *Bataillon de Marche No. 2* captured Jebel Kelb from defending Senegalese troops of the *17e Régiment de Tirailleurs Sénégalais*, but were unable to take Jebel Abou Atriz. Colonel Collet's Circassians were similarly unsuccessful, hitting a wall of Vichy French tanks and artillery fire as they advanced.

Indian, British and Free French troops south of Damascus had made good gains, but encountered strong defences that marked the beginning of the second main phase of the Syria–Lebanon campaign: the Vichy French counter-attack.

THE VICHY FRENCH COUNTER-ATTACK

By mid-June the Allied advance into Vichy-controlled Lebanon and Syria resembled a giant V shape: on the left, the 21st Australian Brigade was at the Mediterranean port city of Sidon; on the right, the combined British, Indian and Free French force was at Kiswe, 5 miles from Damascus; and in the centre, the 25th Australian Brigade had advanced as far as Jezzine and Merdjayoun. The advance had not been as easy as Allied planners had expected, and the Vichy French launched a powerful counter-attack into the flanks of this salient.

The counter-attack plan involved three simultaneous surprise attacks against Allied positions. By attacking key points such as Kuneitra and Ezraa in the east Dentz hoped to cut off Lloyd's Indian and Free French force in the deserts south of Damascus; by taking Merdjayoun, he could disrupt lateral communications between Allied columns and possibly press further south into Palestine; by seizing Jezzine and pressing at an angle towards the coast he could cut the coast road south of Beirut and isolate the 21st Australian Brigade at Sidon. He placed Colonel Amédée Kieme, commander of the Army of the Levant's cavalry, in command of the counter-attack operations.

The Vichy attack in the east

On the afternoon of 15 June Brigadier Lloyd, whose forces were attacking Kiswe south of Damascus, began to receive reports that a Vichy force had advanced from Soueida and captured Ezraa, some 35 miles to his rear. The Vichy Force – five R-35s of the *7e Régiment de Chasseurs d'Afrique* accompanied by Dodge-White armoured cars, a motorized platoon of the *1er Régiment de Spahis Marocains*, a section of the *16e Régiment de Tirailleurs Tunisiens*, with supporting machine guns, artillery and anti-tank weapons – commanded by Colonel Simon, Chief of Staff of cavalry in the Levant, had taken a circuitous route through rocky terrain east of the Deraa–Damascus road and attacked Ezraa from the east.

From there it was well placed to press for the road hub of Sheikh Meskine, but by 16 June, when it made its attack, Brigadier Lloyd had reinforced the Chadian Free French defenders with artillery, and after a hard fight Sheikh Meskine remained in Allied hands. Free French commander Colonel René Génin attempted to exploit his success at Sheikh Meskine on 18 June, attacking with one company to retake Ezraa, but was killed in the fight. Later that day Major J. Winthrop Hackett, an Australian serving in the British Army, scratched together a force drawn from Génin's Free French, a group of Royal Fusiliers who had been guarding Brigadier Lloyd's Headquarters, local Arabic troops, two universal carriers and an anti-tank gun, and took Ezraa in a daring surprise attack. For the loss of 14 casualties – including Hackett, who was wounded in the shoulder – it caused 120 Vichy French casualties, took 170 prisoners and seized a sizeable bounty of enemy materiel.

At the same time that Lloyd heard of the 15 June Vichy attacks at Ezraa, he received reports of a more powerful counter-attack on Kuneitra from the north-east. The threat to Kuneitra was of strategic importance because it was an important road junction linking Sheikh Meskine, Jisr Bennt Jacob (on the Syria–Transjordan border) and Banias (south of Merdjayoun). By taking Kuneitra, the Vichy French could cut communication lines of the central (Merdjayoun) and right (Damascus) attacking columns.

Operation *Exporter*, 8–15 June 1941

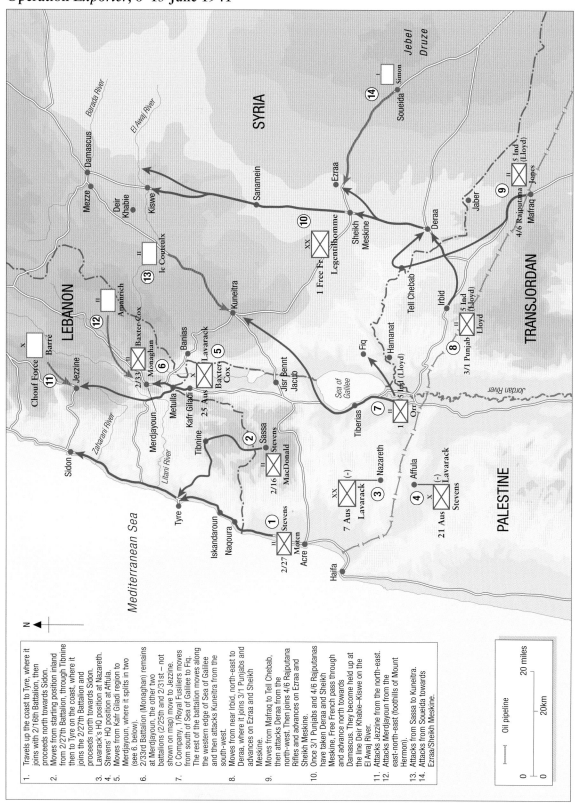

1. Travels up the coast to Tyre, where it joins with 2/16th Battalion, then proceeds north towards Sidon.
2. Moves from starting position inland from 2/27th Battalion, through Tibnine then to Tyre on the coast, where it joins the 2/27th Battalion and proceeds north towards Sidon.
3. Lavarack's HQ position at Nazareth.
4. Stevens' HQ position at Afula.
5. Moves from Kafr Giladi region to Merdjayoun, where it splits in two (see 6, below).
6. 2/33rd Battalion (Monaghan) remains at Merdjayoun, the other two battalions (2/25th and 2/31st – not shown on map) move to Jezzine.
7. C Company, 1/Royal Fusiliers moves from south of Sea of Galilee to Fiq. The rest of the battalion moves along the western edge of Sea of Galilee and then attacks Kuneitra from the south-west.
8. Moves from near Irbid, north-east to Deraa, where it joins 3/1 Punjabs and advances on Ezraa and Sheikh Meskine.
9. Moves from Mafraq to Tell Chebab, then attacks Deraa from the north-west. Then joins 4/6 Rajputana Rifles and advances on Ezraa and Sheikh Meskine.
10. Once 3/1 Punjabs and 4/6 Rajputanas have taken Deraa and Sheikh Meskine, Free French pass through and advance north towards Damascus. They become held up at the line Deir Khabie–Kiswe on the El Awaj River.
11. Attacks Jezzine from the north-east.
12. Attacks Merdjayoun from the east-north-east (foothills of Mount Hermon).
13. Attacks from Sassa to Kuneitra.
14. Attacks from Soueida towards Ezraa/Sheikh Meskine.

In the early hours of 15 June a column consisting of 35 armoured vehicles (a combination of R-35s from the *7e Régiment de Chasseurs d'Afrique* and Panhard 35 TOE armoured cars), one company (about 200 men) from *3e Bataillon, 17e Régiment de Tirailleurs Sénégalais*, Circassian cavalry and four 47mm guns – under command of Colonel Guy Le Couteulx de Caumont – moved out and drove the 1/Royal Fusiliers from their harassing positions near Sassa to Kuneitra. At Sassa it paused to bring large numbers of men, tanks and cavalry into position for a major attack on the more important target of Kuneitra. By the time the attack was ready to begin on the morning of 16 June, the Vichy force numbered some 2,000 troops.

Facing them at Kuneitra were the depleted 1/Royal Fusiliers (less C Company, which was at Kiswe), two armoured cars from the Royal Dragoons and one 20mm Breda gun – about 575 men. Their main defensive line was a 4ft anti-tank wall made of stones. Vichy patrols sent to the Banias, Jisr Bennt Jacob and Sheikh Meskine roads at their rear prevented reinforcement.

The main attack began at 0430hrs on 16 June. The British Breda gun, the only serious defence against the tanks, was mounted on an armoured car, ready for action, but broke a spring and was rendered unusable after firing only five rounds. Vichy tanks were able to operate with impunity and entered the town. Despite desperate attempts to take them out with close-range fire from Boys anti-tank rifles, grenades and Molotov cocktails, nothing could pierce their armour. Dismounted Circassian cavalry accompanying the tanks proved especially difficult – fighting in their market town, they knew the streets and buildings well.

By midday Kuneitra was close to being overrun. Powerful combined infantry and tank assaults forced the remaining Fusiliers to withdraw and join the Battalion Headquarters Company in the south of the town. Corporal Henry Cotton, already a recipient of a Distinguished Conduct Medal for single-handedly attacking a machine-gun post in the Western Desert, rushed forward with two other men to capture an abandoned Hotchkiss gun and ammunition, which he fired against the Vichy attackers for half an hour before it was disabled. He then took a Boys anti-tank rifle, attacked single-handedly and drew fire from French tanks until killed by a round of high-explosive.

The rest of his battalion held on for a few more hours, but by late afternoon were hiding in houses, cut off from ammunition supplies, and surrounded by enemy tanks and infantry. When a Vichy officer approached in an armoured car waving a white handkerchief and told the survivors that they should surrender because he did not like killing Englishmen, the Fusiliers' commanding officer Lieutenant-Colonel Arthur Orr could see the writing on the wall. He surrendered Kuneitra at 1800hrs, and around 180 troops, including 13 officers, were taken prisoner.

The Vichy success at Kuneitra was its greatest of the campaign and was potentially a devastating blow to the Allies. However, it was held for just two days. Colonel Le Couteulx, cognizant of the failure of a smaller Vichy force to capture and hold Sanamein south of Damascus, and fearful of having his tanks surrounded, withdrew with his prisoners to Sassa on the night of 16 June. An Allied force – consisting of C Company, 2/3rd Machine-Gun Battalion (commanded by Lieutenant-Colonel Arthur Blackburn, recipient of the Victoria Cross for his actions during the Battle of Pozières in 1916), a battery of the 2/2nd Anti-Tank Regiment, 60 mounted troops of the

Yorkshire Dragoons and the newly arrived 2nd Battalion of the Queen's Royal Regiment, with artillery support – retook Kuneitra on 17 June with the loss of one casualty.

In the space of four days the Vichy French had launched their major attack, taken targets such as Ezraa and Kuneitra and lost them in short order. The failure to hold these targets and seriously threaten Allied communication lines proved disastrous for the Vichy campaign, not least because Brigadier Lloyd, despite the serious threat to his rear, had decided that the best form of defence was attack. On the night of 15 June he ordered the 5th Indian Brigade to proceed north towards Damascus. Having seized key high ground, by the early hours of 16 June his troops could see the minarets of the ancient city. Not only were they poised to take the Syrian capital, but they had cut the supply lines of Vichy forces attacking further south.

The Vichy attack at Merdjayoun

By the time the Vichy French launched their major counter-attack against Allied forces in the deserts of Syria, the Allies in the central column were split between Merdjayoun and Jezzine. On 14 June Lavarack permitted Lieutenant-Colonel Monaghan, commander of the 2/33rd Battalion, to use one of his companies to make a series of small attacks east of Merdjayoun to seize the Vichy outpost at Hasbaya. Lavarack was quick to remind Monaghan that his main function was to use his limited resources to hold Merdjayoun, and thus protect the right flank of the rest of the 25th Brigade which had advanced towards Jezzine. Monaghan had in effect been granted a free hand for an active defence in the area so long as it did not jeopardize holding Merdjayoun, but the plucky officer, known as 'Mad Monaghan' and 'The Bull' to his men, was frustrated at being left commanding what he saw as a holding force and took a liberal definition of active defence.

On the night of 14/15 June Monaghan sent three companies into the foothills of Mount Hermon with the intention of taking control of the Hasbaya area and cutting Vichy supply lines, leaving one company near Khiam to offer a more traditional defence. When the French launched their powerful counter-attack against Merdjayoun on 15 June, the companies of the 2/33rd Battalion were spread across the mountainous terrain, miles from where they needed to be.

The smaller Allied force at Merdjayoun – one company of the 2/33rd Battalion, 6th Cavalry, Scots Greys, a platoon of machine gunners, two anti-tank guns and the 10th Field Battery – was operating along two roads (dubbed Route 'A' and Route 'B') north of the crusader fort. The Vichy attack began at 1500hrs when two companies of *3e Bataillon, 6e Régiment Étranger d'Infanterie*, mechanized squadrons from the *6e Régiment de Chasseurs d'Afrique*, three squadrons of Circassian cavalry and around 20 R-35s under the command of Colonel Charles Amanrich began moving along Routes 'A' and 'B' and attacking through the rugged hills. The powerful attack forced Allied troops in the area to make a general southward withdrawal over the night of 15/16 June.

A company of the 2/5th Battalion that had been brought into the area to assist in defence and a troop of the Scots Greys were ordered to set up a defensive roadblock to stall the French advance at Merdjayoun while a more extensive defence was established at Qleaa south of the town.

As the 2/5th Field Regiment began to withdraw its guns under heavy fire, a truck driver attempting to avoid a patch of rough ground led the convoy to the bottom of a series of stone terraces about 30 yards wide. The men cut into the terraces to make them passable by truck while hauling the guns up by winch. A French bomber dive-bombed them until a British Bofors gun team 500 yards away opened fire, hitting the aircraft and causing it to crash nearby in a mighty explosion. The Australian gunners stopped to give three cheers to their British saviours and set back to work. By dusk, they had withdrawn through Qleaa as far back as Metulla, just north of the Sea of Galilee, the starting point of the central column's invasion.

The French had achieved considerable successes throughout the day, but failed to capitalize on them. By nightfall on 15 June their attack stalled due to their tanks not being able to operate effectively in darkness. When they did begin a small attack on the Allied defensive line at Qleaa in the early hours the next day, it was met by a heavy and well-coordinated response. This was the extent of the counter-attack in the Merdjayoun area. The fighting was by no means over, but the Vichy French would not penetrate any further south.

The Vichy attack may have petered out, but it was so strong that Lavarack took rapid action. On 15 June he transferred the 2/25th Battalion, the remainder of the 2/5th Field Regiment and a troop of the 2/6th Field Regiment from Jezzine to the beleaguered Merdjayoun sector and placed all troops in the area under command of his impressive divisional artillery commander Brigadier Frank Berryman. By 16 June 'Berryforce' consisted of the Scots Greys, the 2/25th Battalion, the 2/33rd Battalion, the 2/2nd Pioneer Battalion, one company of the 2/5th Battalion and the 6th Cavalry (less two squadrons), as well as machine gunners, artillery and anti-tank troops.

On 17 June Berryman made the first of several Allied attempts to retake Merdjayoun and stifle Vichy French ability to continue aggressive action in the sector. Two companies of the 2/2nd Pioneer Battalion, with artillery support, were to make a frontal assault on the fort from Qleaa while the

A British 40mm Bofors anti-aircraft gun team. (Photo: Frank Hurley, Australian War Memorial, 008794)

47

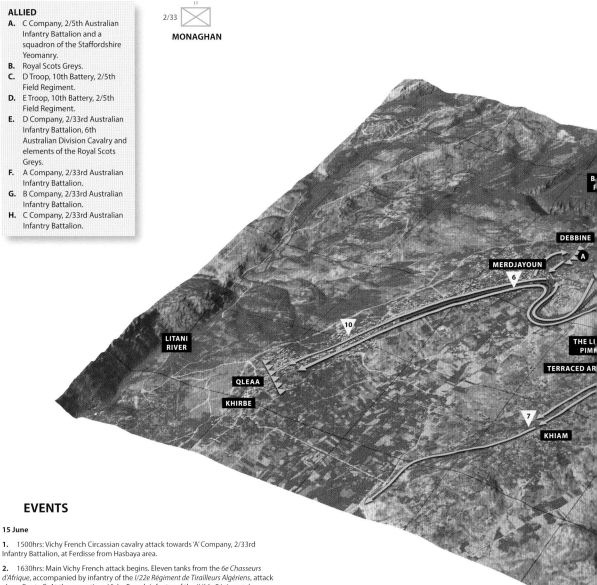

ALLIED

A. C Company, 2/5th Australian Infantry Battalion and a squadron of the Staffordshire Yeomanry.

B. Royal Scots Greys.

C. D Troop, 10th Battery, 2/5th Field Regiment.

D. E Troop, 10th Battery, 2/5th Field Regiment.

E. D Company, 2/33rd Australian Infantry Battalion, 6th Australian Division Cavalry and elements of the Royal Scots Greys.

F. A Company, 2/33rd Australian Infantry Battalion.

G. B Company, 2/33rd Australian Infantry Battalion.

H. C Company, 2/33rd Australian Infantry Battalion.

2/33 ⊠ MONAGHAN

DEBBINE

A

MERDJAYOUN

6

10

LITANI RIVER

B
F

THE LI
PIM

TERRACED AR

QLEAA

KHIRBE

7

KHIAM

EVENTS

15 June

1. 1500hrs: Vichy French Circassian cavalry attack towards 'A' Company, 2/33rd Infantry Battalion, at Ferdisse from Hasbaya area.

2. 1630hrs: Main Vichy French attack begins. Eleven tanks from the *6e Chasseurs d'Afrique*, accompanied by infantry of the *I/22e Régiment de Tirailleurs Algériens*, attack along Route B. At the same time, Vichy French infantry of the *II/16e Régiment de Tirailleurs Tunisiens* and *II/29e Régiment de Tirailleurs Algériens* attack in waves along high ground between routes A and B known as Col's Ridge (informally named after Captain Colin Morris of the 2/5th Field Regiment, killed in action on 13 June). Tanks from the *6e Chasseurs d'Afrique* also attack en masse along Route A. The Vichy column attacking along Route A meets fierce resistance from D Company, 2/33rd Australian Infantry Battalion, elements of the 6th Australian Division Cavalry and the Royal Scots Greys, who, supported by artillery near Ibeles Saki, defend their position astride the road at 'Windy Corner'.

3. 1645hrs: Australian artillery, D and E troops, 10th Battery, 2/5th Field Artillery Regiment, ordered to withdraw south. D Troop moves north to the main road to Merdjayoun, then makes an orderly withdrawal. E Troop moves south along difficult tracks and country towards Khiam. This unit is forced to move its guns and trucks down stone terraces under fire from Vichy aircraft as it proceeds south.

4. 1700hrs: A Company, 2/33rd Battalion withdraws from Ferdisse, through Rachaya el Fokhar, to Bmeriq.

5. Two companies of French infantry drive Allied infantry (two companies of the 2/5th Australian Infantry Battalion) and cavalry (composite unit of troops from the Royal Scots Greys and the Staffordshire Yeomanry) off the Balate Ridge.

6. Retreating Allied units (elements of the 2/5th Australian Infantry Battalion and the Royal Scots Greys) form a roadblock at Merdjayoun to stall the Vichy French advance while other units retreat to Qleaa. This rear-guard is ordered to hold its position until 0245hrs, 16 June, then to withdraw to Qleaa. It successfully holds its position as ordered.

7. 2200hrs: D Company, 2/33rd Battalion withdraws 500 yards from 'Windy Corner' to put rough terrain between its infantry and the oncoming Vichy tanks, then proceeds to Khiam. On entering Khiam the Australians come across a Vichy garrison and take the town and fort in a sharp engagement.

16 June

8. 0530hrs: B Company, 2/33rd Battalion, as yet unhindered by the Vichy French, attacks the Vichy French garrison at Fort Christofini north of Hebbariyeh. The attack is successful, but the company begins to withdraw to Bmeriq at 0700hrs after receiving news of the Vichy counter-attack on the other companies of its battalion.

9. 0630hrs: Vichy French cavalry observed dismounting and preparing to attack C Company, 2/33rd Battalion from the south-east at Rachaya el Fokhar. As the Vichy French attack, B Company, 2/33rd Battalion, on its way to Bmeriq, sees the fight, so manoeuvres behind the French force and attacks their rear.

10. 1030hrs: Two French tanks attack Allied position at Qleaa. The Allied position by this time is Royal Scots Greys on the left, 2/5th Australian Infantry Battalion in the centre and Staffordshire Yeomanry on the right, supported by artillery. One Vichy tank is destroyed and the other withdraws. The Vichy French counter-attack at Merdjayoun has ended.

THE VICHY FRENCH COUNTER-ATTACK AT MERDJAYOUN, 15–16 JUNE 1941

When the Vichy French launched their attack on the Merdjayoun sector on the afternoon of 15 June, Allied forces were spread throughout the surrounding hills. The three battalion-strong attack, supported by tanks and aircraft, sowed panic in the Allied ranks and led to a hasty withdrawal to the south. The Vichy French did not exploit the attack by proceeding further south than Merdjayoun, but by capturing the important town and fort they blocked Allied access to the Bekaa Valley and disrupted Lavarack's plans in other sectors. Merdjayoun would not fall back into Allied hands until 24 June.

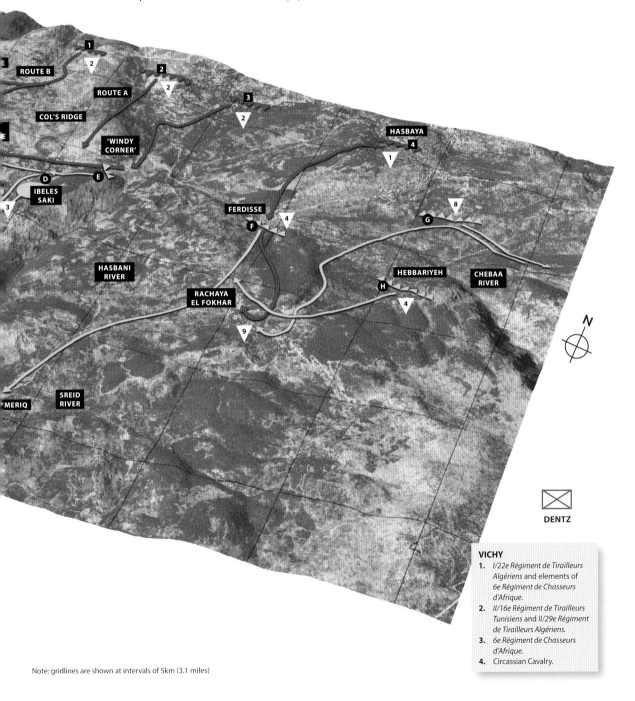

ROUTE B
ROUTE A
COL'S RIDGE
'WINDY CORNER'
D
E
IBELES SAKI
HASBAYA
FERDISSE
F
G
HASBANI RIVER
HEBBARIYEH
CHEBAA RIVER
RACHAYA EL FOKHAR
H
MERIQ
SREID RIVER

DENTZ

VICHY
1. *I/22e Régiment de Tirailleurs Algériens* and elements of *6e Régiment de Chasseurs d'Afrique.*
2. *II/16e Régiment de Tirailleurs Tunisiens* and *II/29e Régiment de Tirailleurs Algériens.*
3. *6e Régiment de Chasseurs d'Afrique.*
4. Circassian Cavalry.

Note: gridlines are shown at intervals of 5km (3.1 miles)

2/25th Battalion moved through the precipitous hills from the direction of Jezzine, across the Litani, and attacked from the north-west. It was a formidable task for the as yet untested 2/2nd Pioneer Battalion, which had not undertaken advance infantry training and, not yet fully equipped, had only one light machine gun and one sub-machine gun per section and no mortars. It was to attack across open ground towards a crusader-era fort with high walls so thick that 25-pdr guns did little damage, facing Foreign Legion troops that knew the country well – *3e Bataillon, 6e Régiment Étranger d'Infanterie.*

The attack was a disaster. As the troops attacked in the darkness of pre-dawn, they came under heavy machine-gun and rifle fire from French troops well positioned behind the stone walls that criss-crossed the area and machine gunners firing from the fort. They suffered terrible casualties before being completely pinned down in wire about 30 yards from the fort. When the sun rose, two French tanks came forward, attacked at will and captured prisoners. Those left on the battlefield spent the rest of the day exposed in the hot sun, lying behind whatever cover they could find. By dusk they had struggled back and established a line 800 yards from the fort, a line that the tanks could not reach owing to anti-tank fire from Qleaa. The two companies of the 2/2nd Pioneer battalion had lost 27 men killed, 46 wounded and 29 taken prisoner.

The 2/25th Battalion never made it to the battle. Throughout the night of 16 June the exhausted men had moved single file through the treacherous mountain passes and waded chest deep through the swift-flowing Litani. At dawn they were approaching the Merdjayoun plateau, but by the time they had reached the upper slopes, all surprise had been lost and they were halted by French defences well short of the fort.

The Vichy attack at Jezzine

As the Vichy French launched their attack at Merdjayoun, the other forces of Brigadier Baxter-Cox's 25th Brigade – the 2/31st Battalion and supporting detachments placed at key positions in the mountainous terrain to the north and south of the picturesque town – came under attack at Jezzine. To their west, the Cheshire Yeomanry held the road linking Jezzine to the coast at Sidon. The Vichy attackers assigned to capture Jezzine, named 'Chouf Force', consisted of *1er Bataillon, 6e Régiment Étranger d'Infanterie*, the *2e* and *3e battaillons* of *17e Régiment de Tirailleurs Sénégalais*, several squadrons of the *4e Régiment de Spahis Tunisiens* and five batteries of artillery, all commanded by *6e Régiment Étranger d'Infanterie*'s Colonel Jean-Luc Barré.

The assault began on the evening of 15 June with a series of probing attacks through the high ground and along key roads. At daybreak on 16 June a Vichy patrol attacked towards Jezzine from the direction of Machrhara but was stopped by a well-concealed Australian company on the road at the foothills of Mount Toumat. The company commander, Captain John Houston, was under instructions – if attacked by a small force – to hold fire enough to capture a prisoner for intelligence. When the Vichy attack was less than 200 yards from Australian positions, Houston's troops opened fire with small arms and an anti-tank gun, hitting three armoured cars, the damaged remains of which formed a useful roadblock as groups of Australians clambered through the hills to take seven prisoners. When another armoured car arrived at the roadblock later in the day and an officer was taken prisoner, Houston joked that he was 'running out of parking space'.

Allied command at Jezzine, October 1941. The precipitous Hill 1284, site of a series of high-altitude battles between Vichy and Allied troops, can be seen in the background. Left to right: Brigadier Jack Stevens, commander 21st Australian Brigade; Brigadier Eric Plant, commander 25th Australian Brigade; Sir Claude Auchinleck, Command-in-Chief, Middle East; Lieutenant-General John Lavarack, commander I Australia Corps; and Brigadier Frank Berryman, commander 7th Australian Division artillery. (Australian War Memorial, 020824)

Throughout 16 and 17 June a series of bitter fights developed around Jezzine, the Vichy French attempting to outflank the defending Australians along key roads and hilly areas. The mountainous terrain was the defining feature of the fighting as each side sought to take the heights that offered commanding views over the enemy. Each hill, named by the Allies according to its height in metres, became a fierce battleground.

A particularly hard fight developed over Hill 1332 on 18 June. The hill, 1.5 miles north-east of Jezzine, offered a particularly good position from which to direct fire on enemy positions. It was taken by an Australian attack during the previous day's skirmishes but was swiftly retaken by a French counter-stroke. At 1050hrs on 18 June, D Company of the 2/31st Battalion began to scale its steep sides with covering fire. When it was 100 yards from the top, the company commander Captain Houston, who had complained of the Vichy French car park developing on nearby roads only days before, fired a Very light signalling for the supporting artillery to stop and for his men to charge. The Vichy defenders waited until the Australians were 50 yards away before opening fire. Seven Australians, including Houston, were killed, and 22 others wounded.

They were not the last to die in the ongoing fight to capture Hill 1332. In the coming weeks Allied and Vichy forces engaged in a bitter fight to secure the high ground and dominate the area. The 18 June attack was a failure for the Australians, but similar to the Vichy stall at Merdjayoun, the French would make no more major advances in the sector. The Vichy French counter-attack was over.

The coastal column

The Vichy counter-attack mostly affected the central and right columns of the Allied attack, but did have the indirect effect of holding up the 21st Australian Brigade's coastal advance. As the powerful Vichy thrusts cut their way through Allied defences further east, Lavarack ordered Brigadier Stevens to stand fast and adopt an aggressive defensive posture until the situation around Merdjayoun had stabilized.

At sea, the Vichy counter-attack occurred at the same time as a flurry of naval activity. On 15 June German dive-bombers attacked and severely damaged HM Ships *Isis* and *Ilex* while Vichy destroyers *Vauquelin* and *Le Chevalier Paul* attempted to bring much-needed ammunition supplies to Beirut. On 16 June *Le Chevalier Paul* came under torpedo attack by six Cyprus-based Fleet Air Arm Swordfish from 815 Squadron north of Rouad Island and sank with the loss of seven lives. *Vauquelin* succeeded in reaching Beirut on 21 June, but was damaged the following day by three Blenheims of No. 11 Squadron, killing five.

Summing up the Vichy counter-attack

The Vichy French counter-attack was short lived but posed a serious threat to Allied command. At the same time that Vichy troops cut off Lloyd's forces in the east, seized Merdjayoun and pressed on Jezzine, significant Allied resources were being devoted to Operation *Battleaxe*, the failed attempt to relieve forces besieged by the Germans at Tobruk. Although distant, Operation *Battleaxe* ensured that already minimal resources, particularly air support, would be diverted further west.

The Vichy counter-attack, or at the least the slower than expected northward advance, also led to an adjustment of the Allied command structure. On 18 June newly promoted Lieutenant-General Lavarack took command of I Australian Corps, in doing so replacing Wilson as commander of Operation *Exporter*.

The shift in command had been intended to occur when the Allied forces reached the Damascus–Beirut road, but given the difficulty of the fight so far it was thought best for Lavarack to assume command earlier than planned. Wilson had been commanding the campaign from his headquarters at the opulent King David Hotel in Jerusalem, and Syria–Lebanon was one of several campaigns occupying his attention. Lavarack's new I Australian Corps Headquarters at Nazareth was much closer to the action; from there he could provide singular focus to the fight.

TAKING DAMASCUS

The Vichy counter-attack of 15 June posed a serious threat to Brigadier Lloyd's rear. If successful, it could sever his already stretched supply lines, which ran from near Damascus to the Palestinian and Transjordanian borders. In response, Lloyd elected to push his forces – the 5th Indian Brigade, Free French allies and a battery of the 1st Field Regiment, Royal Artillery – further north towards Damascus, put pressure on the Vichy French rear and cut the supply lines of the Vichy counter-attackers.

The move had early success. By 16 June the 4/6th Rajputana Rifles and *1er Bataillon d'Infanterie de Marine* had cut Vichy supply lines by occupying a stretch of the Damascus–Kuneitra road around Artouz and the 3/1st Punjab Regiment had captured the high ground of the Jebel Madani. Once in this position, 5th Indian Brigade Headquarters was brought forward to Moukelbe and the Allied force spent 16 and 17 June resting and consolidating – under intermittent and inconsequential Vichy

Circassian cavalry in Damascus, 26 June 1941. (Public Domain)

air and tank attack – for an attack on Damascus planned for the night of 18/19 June.

In preparation for seizing Damascus, the 5th Indian Brigade was ordered to capture Mezze, the western road junction linking Damascus to both Kuneitra and Beirut. The *1er Bataillon d'Infanterie de Marine* was to capture Kadem on the Deraa–Damascus road. At the same time, Colonel Collet's forces further east were to press for Jeremana, capturing the strategically important high ground in that area.

Lloyd's Indian brigade at the time of the attack lacked the 1/Royal Fusiliers, which had been devastated at Kuneitra, and his remaining battalions were below strength. The exhausted and outnumbered troops were to attack powerful enemy positions with a strong enemy force in their rear. It was a gamble, described by historian Gavin Long as 'bold in the extreme, and typical of the irrepressible leader who conceived it', but Lloyd knew that if he succeeded he would stunt the Vichy counter-attack to the south and, by taking the key road junction at Mezze, force the French to retreat along the one road remaining to them towards Homs.

The 5th Indian Brigade set off for a long night march along the Damascus–Kuneitra road on the evening of 18 June, and as it neared Mezze moved away from the road and into the flat countryside to avoid a series of well-defended Vichy roadblocks. The fortified village of Mouadammiye lay in the way, and as the main column passed it in the darkness, it came under heavy fire, sowing confusion in the ranks. The job of silencing the gunners at Mouadammiye fell to A Company, 3/1st Punjabs, while the rest of the attackers – two companies of the 3/1st Punjabs in the front, the Advance Brigade Headquarters in the centre and the 4/6th Rajputanas with sappers and miners and anti-tank troops in support – pressed for Mezze. Among the trees at Mouadammiye the Punjabis threw grenades and yelled to keep in contact, eventually overcoming the powerful Vichy force, including several tanks.

When the 4/6th Rajputanas, now in advance of the main column, reached the outskirts of Mezze, it encountered numerous well-placed Vichy pillboxes.

LAST STAND AT MEZZE (PP. 54–55)

The Indian defenders not killed or taken prisoner as the Vichy French advanced retreated to the Maison Rondeau, the former Syrian headquarters of the British Iraqi Petroleum Company – known at the time as 'Mezze House'. The stately building was surrounded by lush gardens and a high wall. It was also largely surrounded by a deep ravine, rendering it impervious to tanks from three sides. Vichy infantry attacked in waves throughout 19 June with tank support, and the beleaguered Indian defenders – Headquarters Company, 5th Indian Brigade; Headquarters and D Companies, 3/1st Punjabs; and Headquarters and D companies, 4/6th Rajputanas – low on supplies, especially ammunition, fought without rest. The Indian troops successfully destroyed a number of Vichy R-35 with Molotov cocktails (**1**), and defended their increasingly desperate position by firing through holes smashed through the garden walls (**2**).

As the siege wore on, two British officers and a *jamadar* managed to escape under fire to get word of the desperate fight to the Allied command. After an arduous journey, which included crawling through a cactus field in the dark, they were eventually able to reach Lloyd's headquarters, exhausted and bloody, at 0500hrs, 20 June. Lloyd scratched a force together under command of Major Patrick Bourke formed from C Company of the 1/Royal Fusiliers, a rifle company composed of remnant troops of the Punjabis and Rajputanas, two companies of Free French Marines, one battery of the 1st Field Regiment, Royal Artillery and some anti-tank guns, for relief. Despite a desperate fight to reach Mezze, they could not get through the Vichy defences in place along the Damascus–Kuneitra road.

At 1430hrs on 20 June, after more than 30 hours of continuous fighting, the Vichy French brought in 75mm guns (**3**) and blew holes in the walls of the Indian defences (**4**). Shortly afterwards the surviving garrison at Mezze – about 200 men – surrendered. The Vichy troops who entered the Mezze House found it strewn with spent Bren gun and Lee Enfield .303 cartridges, as well as those killed during the battle (**5**). In a few days' fighting at Mezze the bulk of the 5th Indian Brigade, with the exception of a few isolated companies, had been virtually destroyed.

Several accompanying Vichy tanks retired after meeting strong anti-tank fire from the brigade's anti-tank company, and after an hour's heavy fighting the Indian attackers finally overcame the defending unit, the *24e Régiment Mixte Colonial*, took Mezze and some 40 prisoners. The 4/6th Rajputanas set about constructing rudimentary roadblocks in preparation for an expected Vichy counter-attack, while Brigade Headquarters set up in a large building (dubbed 'Mezze House') and a nearby garden.

The fall of Mezze was an important coup for the Allied attackers. On seeing one of their main lines of retreat fall into enemy hands, Vichy commanders in Damascus began to withdraw their troops towards Homs. The French panic was, however, short lived because the planned Free French advance on Kadem, the second prong of the Allied attack, failed to occur. The Free French had fought their way along the Kiswe–Damascus road, and from 15 to 18 June engaged in a fierce fight – including hand-to-hand combat – against their Vichy countrymen over the boulders of the Jebel Kelb, but upon reaching the northern edge of the rocky high ground did not progress any further.

Historians disagree on the reasons for this failure to press on for Kadem. Henri de Wailly's account, which focuses largely on the French perspective of the campaign, attributes the pause to exhaustion. Gavin Long's history of the Australian campaign attributes it to exhaustion and poor morale in the Free French ranks. Dharm Pal's history of the Indian campaign suggests that the Free French flatly refused to advance because they had not received promised air support. His account is damning, but given what was about to happen to the 5th Indian Brigade at Mezze, it is easy to see why the Indian account is less favourable in its assessment of the Free French inability to attack.

Regardless, the failure of the Free French to push north of the Jebel Kelb thwarted the major planned attack on Damascus and, by leaving Kadem in Vichy French hands, allowed the Vichy French to concentrate their forces on a counter-attack at Mezze. That counter-attack came on the morning of 19 June, when large numbers of Vichy tanks from the *7e Régiment de Chasseurs d'Afrique* appeared on the outskirts of Mezze, attacked Indian troops building roadblocks, took prisoners and subjected the survivors to a siege in the urban wasteland (see battlescene artwork, pp. 54–56).

The Vichy success at Mezze, much like success at Kuneitra, was short lived. Allied troops entered the town on the evening of 20 June and found it manned by the dead and dying left behind from the vicious fighting only hours before. The Vichy French had withdrawn to Damascus.

From the middle of June, as the Indians and Free French pushed closer to Damascus, the Allied command decided that the ancient city could finally be taken with the addition of new troops freshly arrived from North Africa. On 18 June Major-General John Evetts, who had recently arrived with the 6th British Division Headquarters, was placed in command of all forces east of the Merdjayoun sector. He soon had under his command the remnants of the 5th Indian Brigade, the newly arrived 16th British Brigade, the 2/3rd Australian Infantry Battalion (still at half strength after fighting in Greece and Crete), the 2/5th Australian Infantry Battalion, the 2/3rd Australian Machine-Gun Battalion and Colonel Casseau's disheartened Free French forces stalled at Jebel Kelb.

The 20th of June proved to be an eventful day on the Damascus front. As the remnants of the 5th Indian Brigade fought desperately at Mezze, with Bourke's force fighting its way forward in an unsuccessful attempt

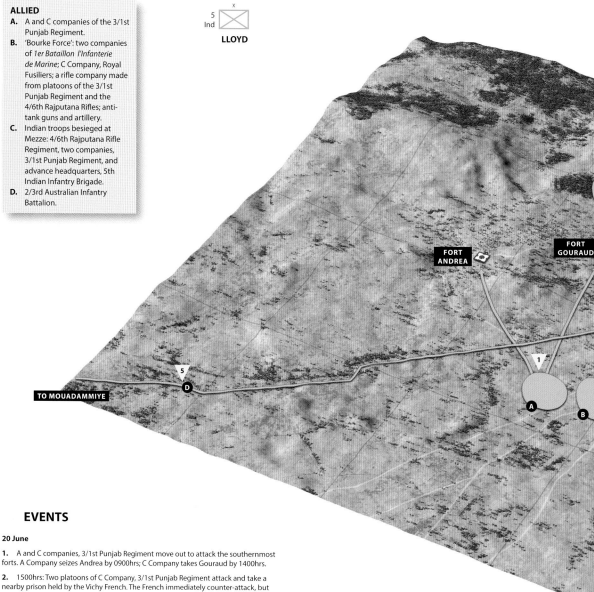

ALLIED

A. A and C companies of the 3/1st Punjab Regiment.

B. 'Bourke Force': two companies of *1er Bataillon l'Infanterie de Marine*; C Company, Royal Fusiliers; a rifle company made from platoons of the 3/1st Punjab Regiment and the 4/6th Rajputana Rifles; anti-tank guns and artillery.

C. Indian troops besieged at Mezze: 4/6th Rajputana Rifle Regiment, two companies, 3/1st Punjab Regiment, and advance headquarters, 5th Indian Infantry Brigade.

D. 2/3rd Australian Infantry Battalion.

5
Ind
LLOYD

FORT ANDREA

FORT GOURAUD

TO MOUADAMMIYE

EVENTS

20 June

1. A and C companies, 3/1st Punjab Regiment move out to attack the southernmost forts. A Company seizes Andrea by 0900hrs; C Company takes Gouraud by 1400hrs.

2. 1500hrs: Two platoons of C Company, 3/1st Punjab Regiment attack and take a nearby prison held by the Vichy French. The French immediately counter-attack, but are repulsed.

3. 1430hrs: Indian forces surrender at Mezze.

4. Bourke Force pushes north to try to relieve besieged Indian forces at Mezze. They reach the outskirts of Mezze in the evening, after the Indians have surrendered.

5. 1730hrs: 2/3rd Australian Infantry Battalion begins forming up for attack on the remaining Vichy-held forts. They begin their attack at 1900hrs.

6. A Company, 2/3rd Battalion is ordered to proceed north, skirt around Mezze and form a roadblock on Damascus–Beirut road; B Company to take Goybet; D Company to take Vallier; HQ Company to take Sarrail.

7. B Company approaches Goybet but is held back by heavy fire from the French garrison.

8. D Company finds Vallier empty, so later sends two platoons to assist in the attack on Goybet.

9. HQ Company successfully takes Sarrail, and at 2000hrs the 2/3rd Battalion commander Lieutenant-Colonel Donald Lamb establishes his headquarters there.

10. Around 2300hrs, HQ Company sends a platoon from Sarrail to the road on the outskirts of Mezze.

11. Vichy French troops of the *III/24e Régiment d'Infanterie Coloniale* move from Kfar Sousa.

12. A Company, 2/3rd Battalion establishes a roadblock on the Damascus–Beirut road and proceeds to hold this position against French attacks from both directions. They capture 26 vehicles and 86 POWs. At first light its commander Captain Philip Parbury leaves one platoon at the roadblock, and moves the rest of his unit up the hill to help take Goybet.

21 June

13. Soon after midnight HQ Company, 2/3rd Battalion sends a patrol from Sarrail, but this almost immediately comes upon Vichy French forces that have moved out from Kfar Sousa. The two groups become engaged in a fierce firefight, and the Vichy French troops eventually push around the Australians and attack Sarrail.

14. Vichy French successfully capture Sarrail and the Australian defenders, including the commander of 2/33rd Battalion, Lieutenant-Colonel Lamb. The Vichy French lead their prisoners down to Weygand. On the way to Weygand they also capture the platoon previously posted to the outskirts of Mezze.

15. 0800hrs: Four Australians in charge of a kitchen truck of the 2/3rd Battalion move out from Mezze to bring food to the battalion. They stop on the road near Weygand, creep up on and kill nearby sentries, free some Australian prisoners being held outside the fort and then lead a small party that captures the fort and releases the rest of the POWs, including Lieutenant-Colonel Lamb.

16. 0930hrs: A and D companies, 2/3rd Battalion attack Goybet, and the Vichy French garrison there surrenders.

THE BATTLE OF DAMASCUS, 20–21 JUNE 1941

The Battle of Damascus was largely fought not in the city itself, but in the surrounding countryside. In the east, Colonel Philibert Collet's Circassian cavalry approached from Jeramana, and in the south Legentilhomme's Free French Division, accompanied by C Company of the 2/3rd Australian Machine-Gun Battalion, approached after a hard fight in the hills near Kiswe. The main action occurred in the west, where a combined force of Indian, British and Australian troops fought to gain control of Mezze and the hills that overlook it. The Vichy French dealt a devastating blow to the 5th Indian Brigade at Mezze, but by 21 June the battle of the hills – and thus the Battle of Damascus – was won by the Allies.

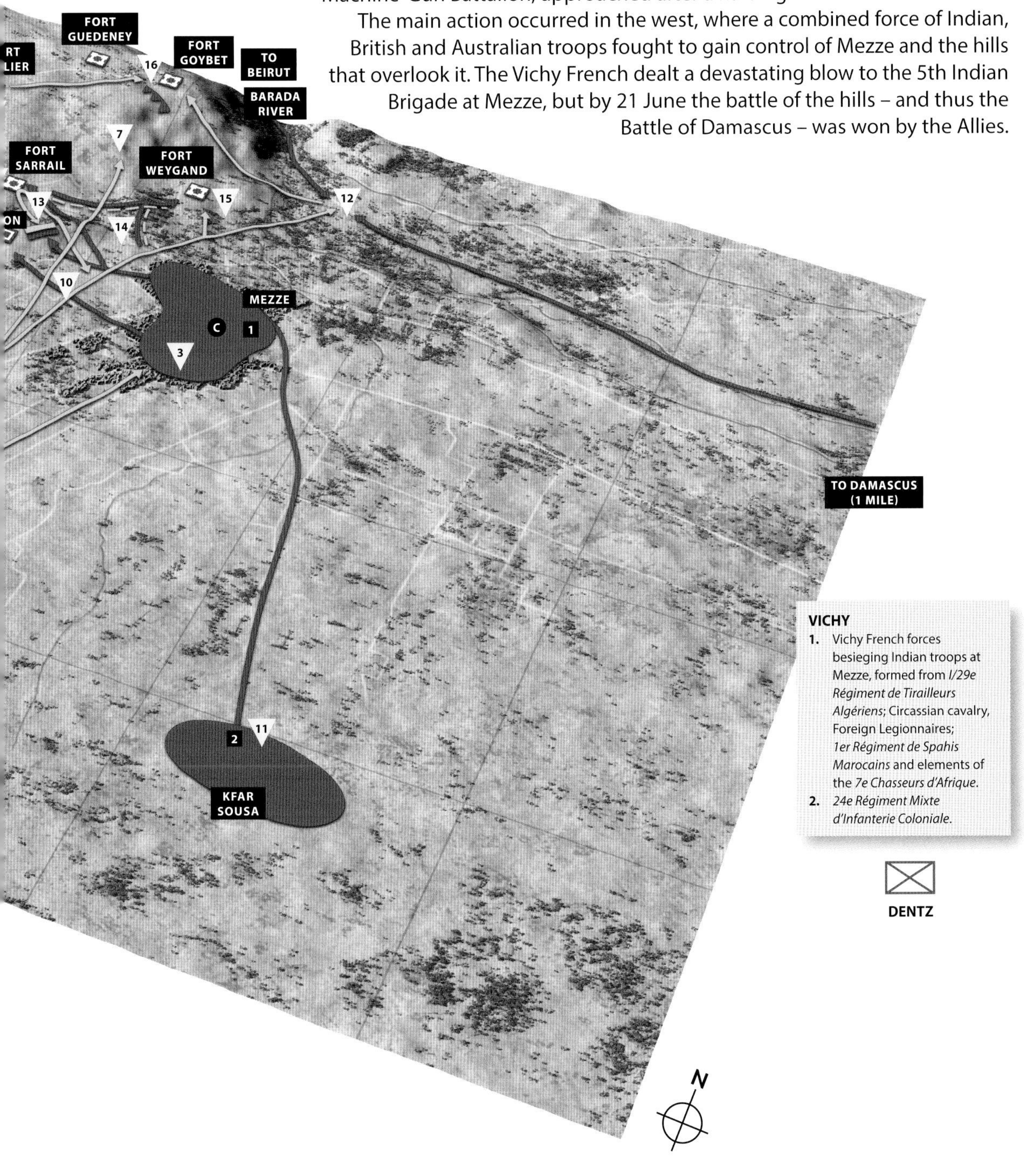

FORT GUEDENEY

RT LIER

FORT GOYBET

16

TO BEIRUT

BARADA RIVER

7

FORT SARRAIL

FORT WEYGAND

ON

13

15

14

12

10

MEZZE

C   1

3

TO DAMASCUS (1 MILE)

11

2

KFAR SOUSA

VICHY

1. Vichy French forces besieging Indian troops at Mezze, formed from *I/29e Régiment de Tirailleurs Algériens*; Circassian cavalry, Foreign Legionnaires; *1er Régiment de Spahis Marocains* and elements of the *7e Chasseurs d'Afrique*.
2. *24e Régiment Mixte d'Infanterie Coloniale.*

⊠

DENTZ

N

Note: gridlines are shown at intervals of 1km (0.62 miles)

to save them, some of Bourke's reserve troops, A and C companies of the 3/1st Punjab, made the first Allied attempt to secure a series of Vichy forts dominating to the west. The seven forts – Andrea, Gouraud, Goybet, Vallier, Weygand, Guedeney and Sarrail, each named after an inspiring French military figure – gave the defender a commanding position overlooking Mezze, the Damascus–Kuneitra road, and most importantly the Barada Gorge, a steep valley along which ran the road linking Damascus to Beirut. Throughout the morning of 20 June two companies of the 3/1st Punjab successfully took the southernmost two of the forts – Andrea and Gouraud – and a nearby prison, before seeing off a determined Vichy counter-attack.

That afternoon Casseau's Free French forces, with spirits boosted by the arrival of elements of Blackburn's 2/3rd Machine-Gun Battalion, again attacked north towards Damascus from the Jebel Kelb. In an effort to inspire the weary Free French, the Australian machine gunners moved in front of the infantry, set up firing positions and waited for the infantry to catch up. Slowly advancing through Vichy artillery bombardment, the combined Australian–Free French force was in the leafy outskirts of Damascus by dusk. The Free French set up defensive positions against increasingly heavy Vichy fire, and the Australians withdrew to form a reserve for the next day's fight.

The next day's fight was concentrated on the hills and forts west of Mezze and the all-important Damascus–Beirut road. After Andrea and Gouraud were captured by the Punjabs, Lloyd sent Lieutenant-Colonel Donald Lamb's depleted 2/3rd Infantry Battalion to capture at least three of the remaining five forts so as to protect the flank of the 3/1st Punjab Regiment attacking Mezze. Lamb allocated a fort to three of his companies and sent Captain Philip Parbury's A Company to trek further north to block the Damascus–Beirut road.

The 2/3rd Battalion began its attack at 1730hrs on 20 June and successfully took forts Vallier and Sarrail, but were unsuccessful at Goybet. At 0400hrs

A British Vickers machine gun overlooking the Barada Gorge. (AirSeaLand Photos)

on 21 June the Vichy French launched a counter-attack and troops of the *3e Bataillon, 24e Régiment Mixte Colonial* retook Fort Sarrail, taking Lamb and his battalion headquarters company prisoner. The Vichy troops marched Lamb and his men towards Fort Weygand, picking up more Australian prisoners along the way as the Vichy-led party came across a roadblock established by some of Lamb's troops the previous day.

The Australians did not remain in Vichy captivity for long. An Australian ration truck manned by Sergeant Carlyle Smith and three others bringing supplies forward was held up by enemy fire, and decided to take a detour towards Fort Weygand. The men crept towards the fort, killed sentries on the outer wall and released one of the imprisoned Australian platoons before attacking the main building of the fort, releasing the Australians and taking the Vichy captors prisoner. The final fort, Goybet, fell around the same time after Lloyd brought in artillery to support an infantry attack.

Free French troops enter Damascus, June 1941. (Keystone-France/Gamma-Rapho via Getty Images)

In the meantime, Parbury's company successfully fought its way to the Damascus–Beirut road where it established a roadblock that captured 26 Vichy French vehicles and nearly 90 prisoners on the roadway.

On 21 June the Allied forces renewed their attack on Damascus: Casseau's Free French force, composed mostly of Senegalese riflemen but supported by Blackburn's 2/3rd Australian Machine-Gun Battalion, renewed its attack from the high ground of the Jebel Kelb; Colonel Collet's Circassians attacked through Jeremana.

By this time the Vichy command had recognized the hopelessness of its position. The majority of Vichy forces in the city were ordered to withdraw at 0800hrs while a small force of Syrian gendarmerie remained to prevent looting. Damascus was declared an open city, and shortly before midday a procession of armoured cars emerged from the city flying a white flag. Casseau and Blackburn drove forward to meet them, and after a brief discussion were escorted to Town Hall by the mayor and his officials. Casseau and Blackburn formally accepted the surrender of Damascus. Hours later Legentilhomme entered the city in a large procession led by Collet's Circassian cavalry.

Damascus had fallen, but the Syria–Lebanon campaign was far from over. The six Vichy French battalions that had withdrawn from the Syrian capital from 21 June – *V/1er Régiment de Tirailleurs Marocains, I/17e Régiment de Tirailleurs Sénégalais, III/17e Régiment de Tirailleurs Sénégalais, III/24e Régiment Mixte Colonial, I/29e Régiment de Tirailleurs Algériens* and *III/29e Régiment de Tirailleurs Algériens* – had made their way west and concentrated in the Anti-Lebanon mountains. There they connected with Vichy forces operating in the north of the Merdjayoun sector and controlled

General Catroux inspecting troops after taking Damascus, 1941. Legentilhomme, his arm still in a sling after being wounded early in the campaign, can be seen in the background. (Keystone-France/Gamma-Rapho via Getty Images)

sections of the Damascus–Beirut road. Further west, the Vichy French continued to aggressively defend at Jezzine and along the coast. In the east, Allied forces were beginning to attack from Iraq.

CONTINUED FIGHTING AT MERDJAYOUN AND JEZZINE

Merdjayoun

The 2/2nd Pioneer Battalion's failed attack on Merdjayoun on 17 June did not dissuade Brigadier Berryman from attempting another. On 19 June – the day that the Vichy French launched their counter-attack on the surrounded Indian forces at Mezze – he ordered the 2/25th Battalion to make a renewed attack from the north-west, this time aimed at the village and connecting roads about 300 yards to the north-east. The 2/25th had formed part of the plan of attack for 17 June, but after traversing precipitous country, bad tracks and the swollen Litani River, were unable to get to the fight on time. They would form the main attack while the 2/2nd Pioneers, supported by the 2/33rd Battalion, the 6th Division Cavalry and a company of the 2/5th Battalion, demonstrated to the south to distract the Vichy defenders.

The two attacking companies of the 2/25th Battalion made initial progress against surprised Vichy troops, the same troops from *3e Bataillon*, *6e Régiment Étranger d'Infanterie*, accompanied by R-35 tanks, who had seen off the 2/2nd Pioneers on 17 June. A hard fight developed amongst the houses of Merdjayoun village and a nearby cemetery. Vichy tanks had superiority and groups of Australians were taken prisoner, but elsewhere the increasingly isolated Australians were able to hold on in small pockets of resistance.

At nightfall Colonel Tony Albord, commander of the Vichy French forces in the Merdjayoun sector, forced the issue by sending in his reserves – the *1er* and *2e bataillons* of the *22e Régiment de Tirailleurs Algériens* and the *2e Bataillon* of the *16e Régiment de Tirailleurs Tunisiens* – for a counter-attack that turned the tide. Shortly after midnight on 20 June the overrun Australians retreated to the Litani River and surrounding areas. Merdjayoun remained in Vichy hands. The Australians had lost more than 20 killed, 50 wounded, 30 missing and at least 50 taken prisoner. The war diary of the 2/25th battalion records the majority of those wounded in action as having been struck by shrapnel and shellfire – this was a battle dominated by artillery and mortar.

From the 19 June attack on Merdjayoun until the end of the month, when the 23rd British Brigade took over operations in the sector, fighting in the area expanded to cover the crusader fort and the important roads and high ground that surrounded it. Vichy forces in the Merdjayoun sector could only be supplied by two major roads, those designated routes 'A' and 'B' by the Allied troops in the first phase of the campaign, so Brigadier Berryman ordered the 2/6th Field Regiment to closely observe and cover Route 'B' to prevent French movement. This left the French with only Route 'A' for supply and possible retreat. Berryman knew that if he could control that road, then Merdjayoun, which had stalled Allied progress in the area since the Vichy retook it in their 15 June counter-attack, would be surrounded, isolated and no longer a thorn in Operation *Exporter*'s side. He also knew that control of that road could be gained by seizing Ibeles Saki and the surrounding foothills of Mount Hermon. An added bonus was that the rugged terrain could not be traversed by the Vichy tanks. He planned an attack for 23 June.

Berryman assigned the task of taking Ibeles Saki to the 2/33rd Battalion and the newly arrived 2nd Battalion, King's Own Royal Regiment. They were to be supported by C Squadron of the 6th Australian Division Cavalry, a mechanized unit whose universal carriers Berryman recognized were unsuited to the rocky country over which they would need to operate. Fortuitously, the 2/33rd Battalion had captured 32 rugged horses from Vichy forces in the area on 16 June, and C Squadron happened to contain many men from the New South Wales countryside who had served in light horse militias in the interwar period. On 22 June they formed an impromptu horsed unit – initially 18- but later 40-men strong – that became informally known as the 'Kelly Gang', named after Ned Kelly, an infamous Australian bushranger (highwayman). For two weeks the Kelly Gang patrolled the area around Merdjayoun, protected the eastern flank of Allied forces in the region, and gathered intelligence on Vichy movements.

On 23 June, as the Kelly Gang set out into the foothills of Mount Hermon, the 2/33rd Battalion and the King's Own began their push towards Ibeles Saki and two nearby high features known as the 'Pimple' and 'Little Pimple'. C Company of the 2/33rd Battalion – now only 73 members strong but supported by a platoon of the 2/3rd Machine-Gun Battalion – attacked Little Pimple behind an artillery barrage in the early morning darkness. On reaching the crest a difficult hand-to-hand fight developed between the Australian attackers and Algerian defenders; the Australians eventually gained the ascendancy.

After initial success on the Little Pimple came the 2/King's Own attack on the Pimple, which was defended by local conscript remnants of the *2e Bataillon, Chasseurs Libanis*. The Lebanese troops put up a stronger than expected resistance and the British troops became pinned down by heavy fire halfway up the hill. Their attack stalled, two companies were left behind to hold their position while the remainder withdrew to prepare for an attack the next day. When they did renew the attack on the morning of 24 June, they came under a confusing barrage of Vichy mortar fire, which killed several men; and when they reached the summit of the Pimple, they found it had been abandoned the previous night. By 0940hrs British and Australian troops had entered their final objective at Ibeles Saki.

By mid-morning it was clear that the French had withdrawn from the area. Hard fighting had been necessary to take the Ibeles Saki ridge, but on 24 June British and Australian units moved forward and occupied several key targets: a patrol from the 2/2nd Pioneer Battalion cautiously entered Merdjayoun fort and found it abandoned, while other Pioneers patrolled the hills immediately north of the fort; troops from the 2/33rd Battalion consolidated control over Khiam, Khirbe and Bmeriq (in addition to Ibeles Saki); the Scots Greys took control around Bourqouz and the Litani River bridge, and had troops patrolling north of Merdjayoun with the Pioneers; and the 6th Australian Division Cavalry commanded the roads connecting the high ground around Ibeles Saki and Merdjayoun.

The Vichy French, under Colonel Albord's orders, had withdrawn to a line running north-east from the high ground north of Merdjayoun to Hasbaya. From this position, their right flank (west) could control Routes 'A' and 'B' while remaining out of Allied artillery range, and their left (east) could prevent the Allies from pushing through the Anti-Lebanon ranges and outflanking them. By late June 1941 the Merdjayoun front appeared much the same as it had on the eve of the Vichy counter-attack weeks before.

From the end of June until the end of the campaign the Merdjayoun sector would cease to be a pivotal area of offensive operations. The Syria–Lebanon campaign had taken far longer than most Allied planners had expected, and General Wavell finally gave Exporter Force the boost in resources that it needed. On 30 June the 23rd British Brigade, under Brigadier Alexander Galloway, took command of the Merdjayoun sector. Allied forces from Merdjayoun to the eastern extremities of the area of operations – including the Free French – were now under command of the 6th Division's Major-General Evetts. The addition of these new units and the change in command structure allowed the entire 7th Australian Division to be concentrated closer to the coast, meaning that the units that had toiled for weeks to try to gain access to the Bekaa Valley shifted west to join the fight around Jezzine and Beirut.

For ten days after the 23rd Brigade took control of the Merdjayoun sector, a tense but stable stand-off emerged between British forces ordered to tie up Vichy forces to prevent them being sent to join the fight on the coast, and Vichy troops content with holding their position and preventing further Allied advances north. The fight continued in the form of near-constant artillery fire and aggressive patrols, but the thrust of the campaign had moved on.

ARTHUR RODEN CUTLER, VC

During the heavy fighting for Merdjayoun on 19 June, 25-year-old Lieutenant Roden Cutler found himself isolated, surrounded by the enemy and hiding in a drainpipe. He had spent the day's battle serving as a forward observer for the 2/5th Field Regiment calling in artillery fire in support of the 2/25th Battalion's initial attack on Merdjayoun town, and throughout the subsequent powerful Vichy counter-attack. When a French tank crew stopped for a cigarette yards away from his hiding place, he hung up his bulky telephone set and hoped no one would call. Once darkness fell, he sneaked back through to the Australian lines, fearing that he would be shot by his own troops as he attempted to do so.

It was the end of a remarkable day for the young New South Welshman – he had mended a vital telephone while under machine-gun fire, personally seen off repeated attacks by tanks and infantry, carried a mortally wounded comrade to relative safety to try and save his life and then gone back into the fray to continue to call in artillery support.

On the night of 23/24 June he oversaw a 25-pdr crew as it brought its gun forward to support the successful attack at Ibeles Saki. During the attack on Damour on 6 July Cutler again became involved in the infantry action, captured eight Vichy prisoners from three separate machine-gun posts and then despite once more being under heavy fire ran forward to ensure that he had a working telephone cable to call in artillery. In this final act he was seriously wounded in the leg. It was more than 24 hours before he could be retrieved from the battlefield, by which time his wounds had become septic. He was evacuated to Yerate, where his leg was amputated as Vichy shells burst nearby.

Cutler was awarded the Victoria Cross 'For most conspicuous and sustained gallantry during the Syrian Campaign'. He died in 2002.

Roden Cutler VC at the cenotaph in Martin Place, Sydney. (Fairfax Media via Getty Images)

The situation changed on 11 July, when the 23rd Brigade advanced north towards the Bekaa Valley only to find enemy positions abandoned. The 23rd Brigade began moving north through the valley towards Bekaa, and although they did not encounter significant Vichy forces, their movement was slowed: retreating Vichy troops had demolished essential infrastructure and left booby traps. The 23rd Brigade was still cautiously making its way north along the Bekaa Valley when a ceasefire brought the campaign to an end at midnight on 12 July.

Jezzine

From 19 June until the end of the campaign the Jezzine front became a fierce battlefield, and despite gains made by each side, the strategic position became a bloody stalemate. The exhausted Vichy and Allied troops in the terraced and rocky hills remained close enough to offer pot shots with their rifles and intermittent mortar and artillery fire, but were so undermanned that little advance was possible. One company of the 2/31st Battalion, for example, was by this stage only 65-men strong, but covered a front of 1,500 yards.

Conditions were made harder for the Allies by the difficulties of getting supplies to the men fighting on the steep hilltops. A ration party took 2½ hours to get from the front lines back to the battalion headquarters at Jezzine, and six hours to climb back, often under Vichy fire. Supply was made even more difficult when on 18 June six Vichy bombers, escorted by fighter aircraft, dropped 20 bombs on Jezzine and scored a number of direct hits on the 2/31st Battalion's rations store at the Hotel Egypt. Forty men were buried in the rubble; most of those killed were the battalion's quartermaster sergeants gathered to draw rations. Coupled with the damage to the main road through town, supply stores and transport equipment, this represented a significant blow to the Allies' ability to supply troops in the area.

The air attack on Jezzine resulted in Lieutenant-Colonel William Cannon, commander of the newly arrived 2/14th Battalion, moving his headquarters, intelligence, transport and supply sections more than a mile to the south. This extended supply lines, and meant that supplies needed to be brought forward along exposed roads well-sited for eager French gunners. Troops bringing supplies forward in trucks had to run a series of gauntlets, the most famous of which was known as the 'Mad Mile'.

The Vichy defenders around Jezzine – *1er Bataillon*, *6e Régiment Étranger d'Infanterie* and *2e Bataillon*, *17e Régiment de Tirailleurs Sénégalais* – do not appear to have had such problems with supply, but intelligence gathered from a Vichy deserter suggested that the heavy fighting had made a serious dent in their morale.

The final stage of the Jezzine battlefront began with a major fight over two features north of the town: Hill 1284 and Hill 1332. The two hills, collectively known as the 'Sphynx', were the main Vichy strongpoints in the area and posed a considerable challenge for any attacker. Each had steep, boulder-strewn and occasionally terraced sides. The west was almost a vertical cliff, while the east was surrounded by a rocky plateau that made frontal assault especially perilous.

The main battle began on 24 June after B and C companies of the 2/14th Battalion, which had taken a circuitous route through Azibibi, began to

The 'Mad Mile', June 1941. The diary of the 2/31st Battalion records the French artillerymen firing more than 300 rounds onto it on 21 June, adding that 'the only result was to make dashing along the road a little more thrilling than usual'. (Australian War Memorial, 023631)

attack from the east. As they clambered down the foothills of Mount Kharat and up the slopes of their objectives, they encountered heavy machine-gun and mortar fire. Advance platoons were able to make small footholds on hills 1284 and 1332, but the supporting platoons became held up in the withering fire. By midday increasingly isolated pockets of Australians – those not killed or taken prisoner – had withdrawn back to the south.

A smaller attack by remaining troops of the 2/14th made around the same time – this time from the south – was similarly unsuccessful. The platoon ascended Hill 1284 – so steep it took them two hours to climb it – and surrounded the stone fort at the top, but after an hour's fight against the determined legionnaires withdrew back down the slope.

Hills 1284 and 1332 once again proved impregnable. In the eight days between 17 and 24 June, the 2/14th and 2/31st battalions lost 44 men killed trying to take them – a serious blow to the already depleted units. When Australian troops occupied Hill 1284 later in the month, they found 21 graves and 15 dead bodies of *1er Bataillon, 6e Régiment Étranger d'Infanterie* defenders. From that point Major-General Allen and Brigadier Eric Plant, who took command of the 25th Brigade on 25 June after Brigadier Baxter-Cox was taken ill, concluded that the best way forward was to avoid similar pitched battles, instead relying on artillery and aggressive patrolling to constantly harass Vichy strongpoints. The Jezzine front became dominated by field guns, and thus it remained until the ceasefire that ended the campaign came into effect on 12 July.

MOPPING UP AROUND DAMASCUS

The fall of Damascus on 21 June was not accompanied by a mass surrender of Vichy troops. Instead, the Vichy forces that had abandoned the Syrian capital mostly moved to the Anti-Lebanon mountains to the west, linked up with Vichy forces fighting near Merdjayoun and took control of key sectors of the Damascus–Beirut road. Other smaller groups marched north towards Homs. This evacuation from the capital meant that if the Allies were to bring an end to the campaign by securing Beirut, they would at the same time need to deal with the sizeable Vichy force in the mountains.

The main task of attacking west from Damascus fell to Brigadier Cyril Lomax's newly arrived 16th British Brigade, composed of the 2nd Battalion, Leicestershire Regiment; 2nd Battalion, Queen's Own Regiment; and the 2/3rd (Australian) Battalion, which had been ordered to transfer from Lloyd's (5th Indian Brigade) to Lomax's command on 23 June. The 2/Leicesters and 2/Queen's Own were ordered to push north-west along the valleys towards Zahle and the Vichy airfield at Rayak, while the Australians were to take the Jebel Mazar, a rocky feature towering 1,600ft above the surrounding country. It was originally thought to be unoccupied, but as the Allies advanced, they encountered fierce enemy defences including tanks and especially accurate artillery being mostly directed from the Jebel Mazar. It did not take long for the Allies to realize that whoever held the Jebel Mazar had commanding views over the surrounding country from which to direct fire, and it became a focus of operations.

One company of the 2/3rd Battalion began to climb the important feature on 24 June, but after being misled by a local guide, on the afternoon of the

Private Clarence Atkinson DCM.
(Photo courtesy Isabella Walker)

following day the men found themselves exposed, under fire, still 500ft below the summit, and two hours' climb from the nearest water source. When Brigadier Lomax heard of their troubles, he allowed another company of the 2/3rd Battalion to assist. This company was misled by the same local guide, and when the men began to climb – in single file because the terrain was so steep – they came under Vichy mortar and machine-gun fire that forced them to take cover amongst the rocks.

On the night of 26/27 June the two companies launched a renewed attack on the summit – their third attempt. The Vichy defenders had the high ground on the steep hill, but they were silhouetted against the night sky and a strong wind masked the sound of the Australian advance. Fierce hand-to-hand fighting ensued, but as dawn began to break, the depleted Vichy battalion fled into the ridges and valleys below, and the two companies of the 2/3rd Battalion took the summit.

Much to their frustration, at the top the Australians found that they did indeed have excellent observation of Vichy positions but lacked an artillery observer to take advantage. Although an observer arrived later in the morning, he had left his bulky wireless set 1,000 yards down in the valley. He never returned after being told to go and collect it.

Throughout 27 June Vichy French troops from *I/17e Régiment de Tirailleurs Sénégalais*, *V/1er Régiment de Tirailleurs Marocains* and *I/24e Régiment Mixte Colonial* made a series of powerful counter-attacks against the outnumbered Allies – the Australians now joined by a platoon from the 2/Queen's Own. The Vichy troops attacked in waves, hiding behind boulders when they could, and as they got closer, employed snipers to take out unsuspecting defenders. During the fight 26-year-old Private Clarence Atkinson of Kogarah, New South Wales charged a Vichy machine-gun post that had pinned down his platoon. Armed with a haversack full of grenades, he darted from rock to rock, hurled his bombs and single-handedly captured the gun. Atkinson was awarded the Distinguished Conduct Medal for his actions, the first known Aboriginal Australian to have received that medal in World War II.

Increasingly surrounded and low on ammunition, the Allies decided to wait until dark and stealthily withdraw down the hill to safety. On the failure to capture Jebel Mazar, Major-General Evetts ordered the 16th Brigade to abandon the attack towards Rayak and move back to the line Deir Qanoun–Yafour – similar to where the three battalions of the 16th Brigade had made their rendezvous on 24 June.

The positions established at this time would remain relatively stable for the next two weeks. By 3 July Evetts had the 1/Royal Fusiliers manning the forts west of Damascus near the Damascus–Beirut road; his 16th Brigade was still deployed from Deir Qanoun to Yafour, forming a north–south line about a mile parallel to the Jebel Mazar; south of that line the remnants of the 5th Indian Brigade held positions on a rocky outcrop called the Col de Yafour; and further west, at Chebaa on the foothills of Mount Hermon facing Merdjayoun, were the North Somerset Yeomanry. These units, along with the 23rd Brigade aggressively patrolling around Merdjayoun, formed a bulwark against any major Vichy plans in the area. By remaining in place, they prevented the French from being able to deploy their troops west to assist in the fight against the Australians advancing on Beirut along the coast.

The relatively static line was broken when the Allies – the 2/King's Own Royal Lancaster Regiment – made a final attack on the Jebel Mazar on 10 July. The 2/King's Own was part of a wider attack being made by the 16th British Brigade (now consisting of the 2/King's Own, the 2/Leicesters and the 2/Queen's Own) and Free French forces, planned to end Vichy domination of the area and assist the Australian advance on Beirut further west.

The 2/King's Own attacked in the early morning darkness. They moved silently across the rocky ground, but once detected by the Vichy French all hell broke loose and the climbing British infantry became trapped by a wall of grenades, mortar fire and tracer bullets. During the fight 24-year-old 2nd Lieutenant Ernest Bailey of Preston, Lancashire used his men to form a human pyramid, allowing him to climb a sheer rocky knoll and attack the French pinning down his men below. Armed with a revolver he shot a Vichy company commander before being bayoneted – the man who killed him was found dead next to his corpse. At daylight the 2/King's Own remained pinned down and digging slit trenches near the summit of the Jebel Mazar, their only help coming from a battery of light mountain guns on loan to the British from the Jammu and Kashmir State Forces which fired on Vichy machine-gun and mortar posts.

The fight on the top of Jebel Mazar lasted for nearly two days. At one point the British were forced to withdraw to a steep side of the summit when two Vichy R-35 tanks unexpectedly appeared on one of the less precipitous sides of the mountain. Unstable on the high ground, the tanks withdrew to flatter country nearby, but took around 90 troops of the exhausted 2/Queen's Own fighting nearby in the process.

They would not remain prisoners of war for long. Amid the bitter fighting of 11 June the Allies received news that a ceasefire was to come into effect at one minute past midnight the following day. The Syria–Lebanon campaign was over.

NORTH SYRIA AND PALMYRA

On 13 June General Wilson ordered Major-General John Clark to prepare his Iraq-based forces to join Operation *Exporter* by invading Syria, seizing the Vichy aerodrome and fort at the ancient city of Palmyra and splitting Vichy forces in half by cutting communications between Homs and the forces concentrated around Damascus and the Bekaa Valley.

The force under Clark's command was Habforce, the group of units assembled in May 1941 to help put down Rashid Ali's Iraqi revolt. By the time it was ordered to attack Palmyra, the force consisted of the 4th Cavalry Brigade (Royal Wiltshire Yeomanry, Warwickshire Yeomanry and the newly mechanized Household Cavalry Regiment); the 1st Battalion, Essex Regiment; elements of 237th and 239th batteries, Royal Artillery; nine cars detached from No. 2 Armoured Car Company, RAF; a battery of 2/1st Australian Anti-Tank Regiment; and the 169th Light Anti-Aircraft battery. Joining them were 350 men of the mechanized Arab Legion, a

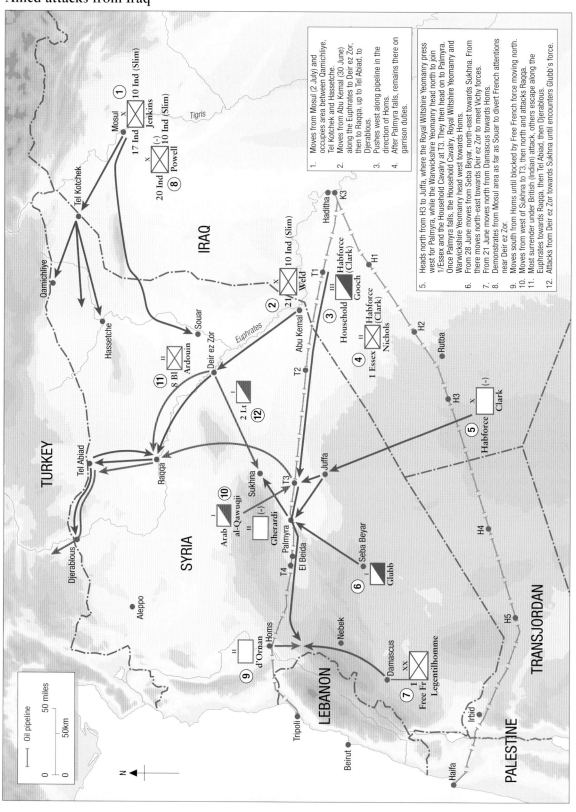

1. Moves from Mosul (2 July) and occupies area between Qamichliye, Tel Kotchek and Hassetche.
2. Moves from Abu Kemal (30 June) along the Euphrates to Deir ez Zor, then to Raqqa, up to Tel Abiad, to Djerablous.
3. Pushes west along pipeline in the direction of Homs.
4. After Palmyra falls, remains there on garrison duties.
5. Heads north from H3 to Juffa, where the Royal Wiltshire Yeomanry press west for Palmyra, while the Warwickshire Yeomanry head north to join 1/Essex and the Household Cavalry at T3. They then head on to Palmyra. Once Palmyra falls, the Household Cavalry, Royal Wiltshire Yeomanry and Warwickshire Yeomanry head west towards Homs.
6. From 28 June moves from Seba Beyar, north-east towards Sukhna. From there moves north-east towards Deir ez Zor to meet Vichy forces.
7. From 21 June moves north from Damascus towards Homs.
8. Demonstrates from Mosul area as far as Souar to divert French attentions near Deir ez Zor.
9. Moves south from Homs until blocked by Free French force moving north.
10. Moves from west of Sukhna to T3, then north and attacks Raqqa.
11. Most surrender under British (Indian) attack, others escape along the Euphrates towards Raqqa, then Tel Abiad, then Djerablous.
12. Attacks from Deir ez Zor towards Sukhna until encounters Glubb's force.

70

mostly Bedouin force offered to the Allied war effort by King Abdullah of Transjordan and commanded by the Briton Major John Glubb of the Royal Engineers, who was affectionately known as 'Glubb Pasha'.

By 17 June the bulk of Habforce's units were assembled at the oil pipeline pumping station H3 (Haifa 3), 140 miles south-east of its target of Palmyra. The Household Cavalry, meanwhile, were based due east of Palmyra at T1 (Tripoli 1) hoping to convince the Vichy French that the Allies were planning to advance up the Euphrates towards Raqqa, and from there onwards to Aleppo.

Typical of the ambitious plans that characterized the Syria–Lebanon campaign, Allied commanders expected Habforce to overrun the Vichy defences at Palmyra in a single day. It was no easy task. The ancient oasis city – which had managed to remain a thorn in the side of both the Roman Empire to its west and the Persians to its east during the 3rd century AD – is surrounded by rocky outcrops and flat salt beds impassable to heavy vehicles. The geography is such that any defender, ancient or modern – in this case about 300 men drawn from *6e Régiment Étranger d'Infanterie*, Bedouins of the *3e Compagnie Légère du Désert* and a small number of air force ground staff – can have a fair idea of the direction from which an attack is likely to come. On top of the natural defences, the Vichy troops could base their operations from a well-defended and heavily wired walled position north-east of the ruins known as Fort Weygand; the eastern approaches were well covered by tank traps, machine-gun posts and snipers; the ruins were riddled with strong positions making use of the ancient columns and stonework; the rocky high ground to the north-west was covered by a 14th-century citadel known as the 'Chateau'; and the south had a good defensive feature in the form of a closely planted pine grove surrounded by 18ft-high walls.

Habforce's attack began on the morning of 21 June. Cavalry columns began racing west to try to surround the Palmyrene defences as quickly as possible. By the end of the first day the Royal Wiltshire Yeomanry gained a precarious foothold on Yellow Ridge, but the Warwickshire Yeomanry pressing north from Juffa was held up by strong fire from the Vichy pillboxes at T3. The Household Cavalry, 1/Essex and remaining artillery marching along the pipeline passed through the pumping station at T2, and, leaving a small force to contain a small piquet of legionnaires, pressed west towards T3. There they joined the Warwickshire Yeomanry in being held up by the Vichy pillboxes, and the advance on Palmyra stalled.

The decisive factor in Habforce's advance on Palmyra, and the main reason for the failure to capture Palmyra in a single day, was Vichy air superiority. On 21 June the Vichy command in Beirut received reports that Habforce was on the march and decided to focus its available air assets on attacking the desert column. The Vichy French made their first attacks from around midday on 21 June, conducting bombing raids on Allied positions at T3 and on Yellow Ridge with twin-engined LeO 451 medium bombers of *Groupe de bombardement I/25, I/31* and *I/12*. The following day available

Glubb Pasha was well respected by the Arab troops under his command. As they went into battle, they cried *'Abu Haneik!'* (literally, 'Father of the little jaw!'), a reference to Glubb's deformed chin, a souvenir from the 1917 Battle of Passchendaele. (Keystone-France/Gamma-Keystone via Getty Images)

AIR FIGHT OVER PALMYRA (PP. 72–73)

A major success for the Allies in the air came on 28 June, after six Glenn Martin 167F bombers of *Flotille 4F* made two separate bombing raids in central Syria: one on British troops south-east of Palmyra (*Groupe de bombardement I* – consisting of two aircraft), the other on British forces north of Palmyra (*Groupe de bombardement 2* consisting of four aircraft). Nine Tomahawks of No. 3 Squadron, RAAF, saw the explosions caused by the French attack as they returned to base having escorted raiding RAF Bristol Blenheims, and engaged the enemy aircraft. The six Vichy bombers, which had attacked in pairs, were all shot down. None of the Australian aircraft sustained damage.

Flight Lieutenant Alan Rawlinson in his Curtiss IIB (P40-B) Tomahawk (serial number AK 446) of No. 3 Squadron, RAAF (**1**), is depicted destroying *Groupe de bombardement 2 Aéronavale* (Fleet Air Arm) *Lieutenant de Vaisseau* François Xavier Paul Martial Ziégler's Glenn Martin 167F 6B-3 of Flotille 4F (**2**) in the skies near Palmyra (**3**).

Lieutenant de Vaisseau de Gail's Glenn Martin 167F 7B-3 (**4**) was shot down in the action. *Sous Maître* Sarrotte and *Sous Maître* Gueret were the only survivors. *Enseigne de Vaisseau* Playe's Glenn Martin 167F 6B-4 (**5**) was destroyed with a total loss of life. Sergeant Mervyn Baillie, who flew Curtiss IIB (P40B) Tomahawk AK 420 (**6**) in the action, would later be killed in an aircraft accident on 11 April 1942 while serving as an instructor with No. 1 Middle East Training School (Conversion and Refresher School), RAF in Egypt.

Although the successful action on 28 June 1941 did not completely bring an end to Vichy air attacks, it did result in a significant reduction in the intensity of Vichy attacks on the desert columns. Rather than strafing Allied columns, Vichy fighters now escorted bombers and remained at a high altitude to watch for enemy fighter attacks.

Vichy fighters and bombers, including *Flotille 4F* of the *Aéronavale*, were thrown into the fight. On 22 June the Vichy *Aéronavale* and *Armée de l'Air* collectively flew 122 sorties against Habforce. The Vichy attacks, chiefly carried out by Glenn Martin 167Fs, Morane–Saulnier MS.406s and Dewoitine D.520s – assisted by considerably slower 1920s-era Potez 25 biplanes – disrupted supply and sowed panic in the lines. One troop of the Wiltshire Yeomanry lost 13 of its 17 vehicles during the attacks. Between 21 June and 3 July the Vichy French carried out some 419 bomber and fighter sorties over the Allied forces attacking Palmyra – a considerable concentration of air power on a relatively small target.

Vichy airmen were able to enjoy unmatched success in the skies over Palmyra because Allied air power for the most part remained tied up protecting the fleet off the coast. The constraint on resources resulted in Air Commodore Brown deciding to dull the Vichy air threat over Habforce not by engaging in dogfights, but by focusing on destroying Vichy aircraft on the ground. The first such attack came on 23 June when six Hurricanes of No. 80 Squadron and four from No. 260/450 Squadron attacked Baalbek airfield 30 miles north of Damascus, destroyed four Martin 167Fs on the ground and damaged several others. The Hurricanes – one piloted by Roald Dahl – proceeded south-west to Rayak where they engaged in a dogfight with Dewoitine fighters of *Groupe de chasse III/6*, which had been alerted to the coming Hurricanes and taken off in time to avoid destruction on the ground. In the ensuing fight the Vichy French reported shooting down five Hurricanes. Later in the day 12 Tomahawks of No. 3 Squadron RAAF attacked the undefended Kuseir airfield near Aleppo, and on return to base engaged Vichy Dewoitines in the skies 20 miles east of Beirut at Zahle, destroying two without loss.

The Allied plan to attack Vichy aircraft on the ground proved a successful tactic, reducing enemy air capability in the battle for Palmyra and the campaign as a whole. General Jean Jeannekyn, commander of the Vichy air force in the Levant, later stated that Allied air attacks on Vichy bases had decided the fate of French resistance. The constant attacks forced him to base his airfields far behind Vichy troops and significantly reduced the superiority in numbers that he had enjoyed at the beginning of June 1941.

Beneath the unfolding air battle on 22 June Habforce was still held up in the deserts east of Palmyra. For the next week Major-General Clark, whose advance Divisional Headquarters was now based in the Juffa area, used all of Habforce's units in repeated attacks, each one held up by the combination of heavy Vichy ground defences and attacks from the air: the Household Cavalry became involved in a deadly stalemate in the rocky ground north of Palmyra; the Royal Wiltshire Yeomanry held its precarious foothold on Yellow Ridge but was subject to frequent air attack; the Warwickshire Yeomanry, trying to push west and make contact with the Royal Wiltshires, could not break through, mostly because of frequent air attacks that destroyed fuel and water trucks.

On 28 June, the day that the Allies wrested control of the skies from Vichy airmen, the Royal Wiltshire Yeomanry made considerable gains to take control of the Yellow Ridge, and a company of the 1/Essex Regiment captured the Chateau north-west of Palmyra. The medieval fort, which had poured devastating fire on Allies and held up their attacks for a week, was captured with relative ease – six of the defenders were captured while

The Battle of Palmyra, 21 June–4 July 1941

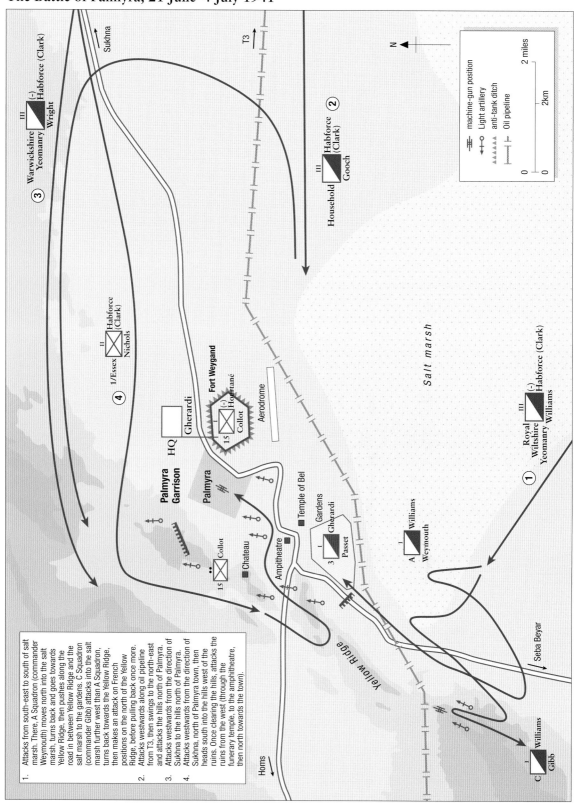

1. Attacks from south-east to south of salt marsh. There, A Squadron (commander Weymouth) moves north into the salt marsh, turns back and goes towards Yellow Ridge, then pushes along the road in between Yellow Ridge and the salt marsh to the gardens. C Squadron (commander Gibb) attacks into the salt marsh further west than A Squadron, turns back towards the Yellow Ridge, then makes an attack on French positions on the north of the Yellow Ridge, before pulling back once more.
2. Attacks westwards along oil pipeline from T3, then swings to the north-east and attacks the hills north of Palmyra.
3. Attacks westwards from the direction of Sukhna to the hills north of Palmyra.
4. Attacks westwards from the direction of Sukhna, north of Palmyra town, then heads south into the hills west of the ruins. Once clearing the hills, attacks the ruins from the west (through the funerary temple, to the amphitheatre, then north towards the town).

asleep. On 29 June Vichy Legionnaires made a determined counter-attack that retook Yellow Ridge from the Royal Wiltshires, but by the following day themselves were subject to heavy British artillery fire and an attack from the north by the 1/Essex Regiment. Palmyra was slowly being surrounded – the Allies had gained the ascendancy.

As the British units slowly closed around Palmyra in what Churchill referred to as the 'ring of steel', Arab forces fighting for each side extended the area of battle further afield, into the deserts of Syria. Arab nationalist leader Fawzi al-Qawuqji's irregular troops attached to Vichy forces in the area employed guerrilla tactics to harass British units to the east, especially along the oil pipeline running from Iraq to the Mediterranean coast. On 24 June several of al-Qawuqji's trucks approached a small group of Warwickshire Yeomanry near the T3 pumping station bearing white flags and proceeded to open fire on the men who emerged from their defensive positions to parley. Twenty-two British were killed, wounded or captured. Vichy officers captured later in the campaign insisted that the white flags were not a symbol of truce but rather a means of identification employed by the Vichy French to avoid attack from their own aircraft. That some reports state that an Arab leader – possibly al-Qawuqji – came forward to parley before opening fire casts doubt on the French assertion.

Glubb Pasha's Arab Legion patrolled the surrounding deserts, and in many ways its efforts were the catalyst for the Vichy garrison's surrender at Palmyra. On 28 June it helped shore up Habforce's supply lines to the south by taking Seba Beyar, and on 29 June it occupied Sukhna, north-east

British universal carriers in Palmyra. 'The Chateau' can be seen in the background. (© Imperial War Museum, E4091)

Searching for snipers in the ruins of Palmyra, 12 July 1941. (Public Domain)

of Palmyra on the road to Deir ez Zor, an important hub on the Euphrates. Two days later Glubb's forces were patrolling in the mountain passes to the north when, as they ate their breakfast, they noticed a column of dust coming from the direction of Deir ez Zor: Bedouin troops of the *2e Compagnie Légère du Désert* were racing south to put an end to Glubb's raids.

Less than half a mile from Glubb's patrol of 30 infantry and armoured cars, the Vichy French dismounted and attacked on foot. Glubb ordered his men to hold fast, but his Bedouin troops could not resist charging, cornering the alarmed enemy in a valley, and capturing 80 men, five officers, six armoured cars, two trucks and 12 machine guns.

Glubb's men had pulled off a remarkable local victory that had far-reaching consequences. On hearing of the fate of their comrades near Sukhna, the remnants of the besieged *3e Compagnie Légère du Désert* at Palmyra deserted in droves. This reduced the defenders' numbers almost by half, and was the final blow to the Legionnaires' hopes of continued resistance. On 3 July the Palmyra garrison at Fort Weygand surrendered. By that point, the garrison numbered only 165 men: six French officers, 87 Germans and Russians of the Foreign Legion, 48 men of the air force and 24 loyal troops of the *3e Compagnie Légère du Désert*. The following day the 22 men holding out at T3 followed suit. Collectively, they had held out against far superior Allied forces for 12 days with dwindling supplies. One can only guess how the Germans and Russians felt fighting side by side in the Syrian desert – on 22 June, a day after Habforce launched its attack, Hitler had invaded the Soviet Union.

After capturing Palmyra, Habforce's cavalry (the 1/Essex Regiment was left on garrison duties) pushed west towards Homs to tighten the noose and prevent Vichy forces from retreating from the Bekaa Valley or coastal areas. On 6 July the cavalry moved to El Beida and by 11 July, as the campaign came to an end, met up with a Free French force south of Homs. Supported by British artillery and an Australian cavalry unit, the Free French force had pushed north into the area in the days after the fall of Damascus, encountering pockets of Vichy resistance, including a tank and infantry counter-attack on Nebek on 30 June. For the most part, however, they conducted patrols to restrict Vichy movement behind the lines of the larger fight developing on the coast.

ATTACKS ALONG THE EUPHRATES

On 21 June Major-General William Slim, commander of the 10th Indian Division which had taken over garrison duties in Iraq from Habforce, received orders to concentrate a force at Haditha and advance up the Euphrates to Aleppo. The attack formed part of the larger Allied plan to threaten the rear of Vichy forces operating further south, especially in Beirut. Slim moved the 21st and 25th Indian Infantry Brigade groups to Abu Kemal, from where they would advance on Aleppo via Deir ez Zor, the regional capital and home to a French-built bridge over the Euphrates. The 20th Indian Infantry Brigade Group moved to Mosul, from where they would feign an attack towards Deir ez Zor, acting as a diversion to the Vichy French defenders. As was the case for Habforce, the 10th Indian Division would have to operate in an area where the Vichy French had air superiority; its only air support came from an improvised squadron of four Hurricanes and four Gladiators from No. 127 Squadron RAF.

The 21st Brigade Group, which formed the main striking force, advanced on Deir ez Zor on 30 June, attacking in three columns following the Euphrates River and pipelines close to its west. The initial advance was held up by poor roads, long stretches of desert, difficulties in water supply and a severe dust storm that prevented significant movement. It was not until the early morning of 3 July that the main attack began: 'Nibe Column' (2/10th Princess Mary's Own Gurkha Rifles and artillery) making a frontal attack from the south-east along the Euphrates; 'Puna Column' (4/13th Frontier Force Rifles, 13th Duke of Connaught's Own Lancers [less one squadron] and artillery) moving around the west of the town so as to make an attack from the north; 'Fund Column' (two companies of the 2/14th Gurkha Rifles and artillery) following up 4 miles behind Nibe Column.

Indian troops met stiff resistance from accurate Vichy 75mm guns and machine-gun positions, mostly manned by local Syrian troops. Ten Vichy bombers with fighter support appeared over the battlefield at about 1100hrs and caused casualties in the Allied lines. The Allies pushed forward, and at midday, after more than six hours fighting, the 2/10th Princess Mary's Own Gurkha Rifles saw armoured cars of the 13th Duke of Connaught's Own Lancers moving through Deir ez Zor from their northern flanking position making it clear that the town was in Indian hands. Troops of the 21st Indian Brigade Group took the town, about 100 prisoners, nine guns, five aircraft and large numbers of trucks, machine guns, rifles and ammunition.

The main cause of consternation for Allied troops operating in the Syrian desert was incessant Vichy air attacks. Strafing men and supply columns, these attacks destroyed large weapons dumps, but owing to well-dug slit trenches left behind by the Vichy French, caused relatively few casualties in Indian lines. The limited available air support unsuccessfully attempted to stem the flow of Vichy air attacks; by 6 July all four supporting Hurricanes had been shot down.

On 5 July the 2/4th Prince of Wales' Own Gurkha Rifles and the 13th Duke of Connaught's Own Lancers with supporting artillery moved 90 miles north-west from Deir ez Zor to Raqqa, and three days later directly north to Tel Abiad on the Syrian–Turkish border. Cutting off the retreat of Vichy forces escaping Habforce further to the south, when they arrived on 9 July they found Tel Abiad abandoned. A squadron of the Lancers' armoured cars and one company of the 2/4th Gurkhas chased retreating Vichy troops to the Turkish border at Djerablous, skirmishing with rear-guard Vichy troops escaping over the Euphrates. As always, the main cause of concern for the Allies was near-constant Vichy air raids, which caused havoc among supply columns and the morale of the men on the ground.

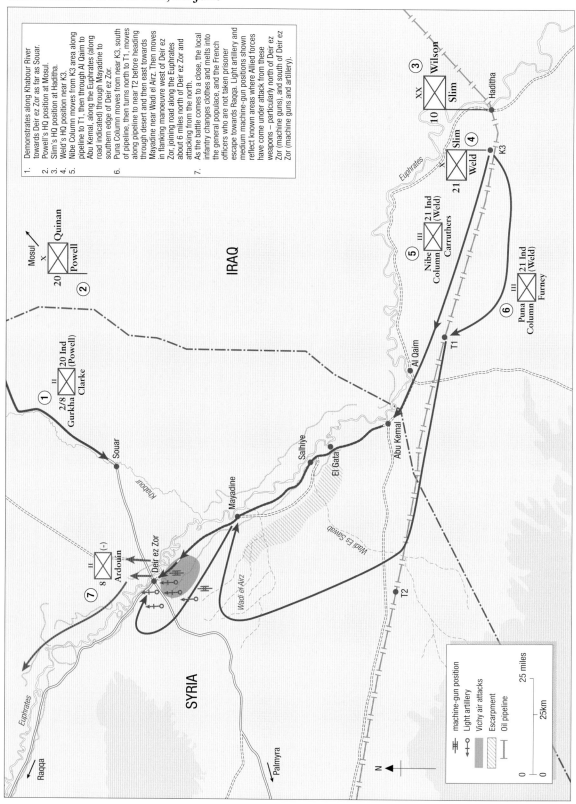

1. Demonstrates along Khabour River towards Deir ez Zor as far as Souar. Powell's HQ position at Mosul.
2. Slim's HQ position at Haditha.
3. Weld's HQ position near K3.
4. Nibe Column moves from K3 area along pipeline to T1, then through Al Qaim to Abu Kemal, along the Euphrates (along road indicated) through Mayadine to southern edge of Deir ez Zor.
5. Puna Column moves from near K3, south of pipeline, then turns north to T1, moves along pipeline to near T2 before heading through desert and then east towards Mayadine near Wadi el Airz. Then moves in flanking manoeuvre west of Deir ez Zor, joining road along the Euphrates about 6 miles north of Deir ez Zor and attacking from the north.
6. As the battle comes to a close, the local infantry changes clothes and melts into the general populace, and the French officers escape towards Raqqa. Light artillery and medium machine-gun positions shown reflect known areas where Allied forces have come under attack from these weapons – particularly north of Deir ez Zor (machine guns), and south of Deir ez Zor (machine guns and artillery).

A powerful Vichy counter-attack on the small force of Gurkhas and Frontier Force Rifles garrisoning Raqqa made mainly by al-Qawuqji's Arab nationalists – machine-gun and artillery fire along the Euphrates, air attacks and raids into the town and on supply columns – caused light casualties, but destroyed 1,500 gallons of petrol stored in the town, a significant blow to the scant supplies available to Slim's men in the area. Sporadic fighting – except for the air attacks, which remained constant – continued until 12 July when the bulk of the force returned from Tel Abiad.

As the 10th Indian Division advanced towards Aleppo, the 17th Indian Infantry Brigade (of the 8th Indian Division) advanced from Basra and through Mosul (where the 10th Indian Division's 20th Brigade Group remained based) to operate in Syria's extreme north-east – the area Qamichliye–Demir Kapou–Tel Kotchek–Hassetche. From 2 July until the end of the campaign units of the 17th Indian Infantry Brigade spread out along the difficult roads and tracks of the region and occupied the various towns and Vichy garrisons without opposition. The official history of the Indian armed forces in World War II notes that the troops that pushed into Syria from Iraq lacked opportunities for 'covering themselves in glory' like their comrades who assaulted Damascus, but nonetheless did their part in difficult circumstances, and by securing their corner of Syria contributed to the Allied pressure that forced Dentz to surrender.

THE FINAL PUSH ON THE COAST

While the Vichy counter-attack of 15 June mostly affected the central and right columns of the Allied attack, it also held up the 21st Australian Brigade's coastal advance. As powerful French thrusts cut their way through Allied defences further east, Major-General Lavarack ordered Brigadier Stevens to stand fast and adopt an aggressive defensive posture until the situation around Merdjayoun had stabilized: the Vichy counter-attack threatened the coastal column's flank, and to advance further north would expose their supply lines further.

Unable to press on, the 21st Australian Brigade settled in to a period of what Gavin Long's history of Australian operations in Syria–Lebanon describes as 'aggressive patrolling'. This is something of an understatement. From 18 June until the end of the month Brigadier Stevens' units – principally the 2/16th Battalion, the 2/27th Battalion and the 2/25th Battalion supported by the 9th Australian Division Cavalry, the 6th Australian Division Cavalry, the Cheshire Yeomanry and artillery – fought in a series of sharp engagements against Vichy roadblocks and strongpoints along the coastal plain from the Wadi Zeini to Es Saadiyate, and in the hills running parallel to the coast to a depth of about 10 miles.

The general move north was conducted in preparation for the coming fight along the Damour River, the last main line of Vichy defences before the Allies could attack the main military base and administrative capital of Lebanon and Syria at Beirut. The Allied tasks were to clear the coastal area of enemy troops, establish positions south of Damour River from which enemy positions and defences could be observed and reconnoitre river crossings from which to launch the attack. This last task was particularly important as the Vichy defensive units – *II/6e Régiment Étranger d'Infanterie, II/22e Régiment de Tirailleurs Algériens*, tanks of the *6e Régiment de Chasseurs d'Afrique* and artillery – had been organized along the north bank of the river in preparation for a likely attack.

The Vichy units had been in the area since 17 June and used that time to build up formidable defences, including extensive covered trenches, well-camouflaged machine-gun positions amongst the rocky outcrops and barbed-wire entanglements. They had spent weeks ranging their guns, mortars and artillery, focusing on likely river crossings, and had blown the one bridge in the area.

While the 2/16th and 2/27th battalions prepared Allied positions closer to the coast, the 2/25th Battalion fought its way through the hills further

The steep-sided Damour River valley. Attacking troops needed to clamber down the south side and climb the north during the 7th Australian Division's attack. (Library of Congress, Public Domain)

inland. On 25 June Allen ordered the 2/25th Battalion, supported by an anti-tank gun and artillery, to patrol east from the Sebline area to Chehim, Daraya, Aanout, El Mtoulle and Hasrout and occupy high ground offering commanding views of roads leading to Beit ed Dine to the north. Control of Beit ed Dine and the surrounding countryside was essential for the success of the Battle of Damour developing on the coast: an important road junction and Vichy strongpoint, if the Allies did not control it then the French would be able to bring in troops to turn the tables in the fight near Beirut.

The march inland was gruelling. The men made their way along tracks so rough that the mules carrying mortars had to be left behind, avoiding pockets of Vichy resistance such as the small unit holed up at Mazboud which had fired on a Cheshire Yeomanry patrol days before. Two companies of the 2/2nd Pioneer Battalion, recently brought to the coast after being relieved by 1st Battalion of the Durham Light Infantry at Merdjayoun, moved into the area to offer support. By 10 July the 2/25th and 2/2nd Pioneer battalions, with artillery support, had cleared the Vichy French from the hills around Mazraat Ech Chouf – high ground that offered an excellent position from which to direct artillery fire into the surrounding countryside.

The 2/25th and 2/2nd Pioneer battalion's attack formed one of two columns advancing on Beit ed Dine. As the 2/25th moved east from the coast, the 2/31st Battalion and supporting troops, including the horsed Cheshire Yeomanry, moved north from the battlefield at Jezzine towards the same target.

On 9–10 July D Company of the 2/31st Battalion made an attack on high ground at Badarane, a position that offered good views over the Beit ed Dine–Jezzine road. This was one of the most physically demanding tasks of the campaign. To reach their objective, the men had to climb down a steep 800ft wall and cross a wadi before climbing 600ft up a series of high terraces into the face of strong Vichy defences.

Setting out along winding paths in the bright moonlight of 9 July, in the early hours of the next morning the men came under heavy fire from Vichy machine-gun positions on the Badarane heights. Clambering through

PRIVATE JIM GORDON VC

In the early hours of 10 July 1941, a concealed and accurate Vichy machine-gun position pinned down a number of men among the olive trees and terraces of the Badarane heights. With his platoon unable to move, 32-year-old Private Jim Gordon exclaimed 'Blast it, here goes!', and crawled towards the enemy as bullets and grenades landed around him. Close to the machine-gun nest he jumped to his feet, charged the enemy position and single-handedly killed the four Senegalese defenders with his bayonet.

Gordon was awarded the Victoria Cross for his actions at Badarane, his citation stating that his actions 'completely demoralized the enemy in this sector' and allowed his company to advance.

A farmer from Rockingham, Western Australia, Gordon enlisted in the Second Australian Imperial Force in April 1940 and joined the 2/31st Battalion in March 1941. He later said, 'The VC is a funny thing. There is only one that gets it, but 20 around you know that should'.

War artist William Dargie, who painted Gordon's portrait in December 1941, later described him as 'not the smiling, happy-go-lucky Digger of legend … I noticed he was trembling.

Corporal Jim Gordon VC, having his portrait painted by William Dargie. (Australian War Memorial, 022350)

Thinking he was feeling the strain of the pose, I said, "Have a rest. I've had you sitting too long." "No, that's alright," he said. "I always get like this when I think of that action."

an olive grove and up a nearby terrace they engaged in a heavy fight until 0500hrs, by which time some 13 Australians and an estimated 50 Senegalese defenders were killed or wounded. The exhausted men, low on food and ammunition, remained on the Badarane heights for two hours before being ordered to destroy all Vichy equipment they could find and withdraw. The Vichy French were organizing a counter-attack and the Australian position was becoming increasingly hopeless.

The two-pronged advance towards Beit ed Dine, despite failing to reach its final objective before the campaign came to an end, prevented Vichy movements in the mountainous terrain inland from Beirut where a much larger battle – the final major action of the campaign – was taking place.

THE BATTLE OF DAMOUR

The Vichy counter-attack of mid-June frustrated Operation *Exporter*'s coastal attack by drawing resources to the east, and it was not until Allied command were satisfied that the situation had stabilized on the Merdjayoun front that they decided to recommence the northward march. By the time this decision was made, the addition of new units to the campaign allowed the 7th Australian Division to concentrate in the area to overwhelm Vichy defences. From the end of June the 21st Australian Infantry Brigade, which was already on the coast, was joined by the 6th Australian Division's 17th Brigade – scratched together from the 2/3rd, 2/5th and 2/2nd Pioneer battalions – and the 25th Brigade, which had been occupying the Merdjayoun sector until relieved by the 23rd British Brigade.

On 4 July Major-General Allen, who had commanded the 7th Australian Division after Lavarack's elevation to command I Australia Corps, issued a plan: the 2/16th Battalion was to make a frontal attack near the coast at

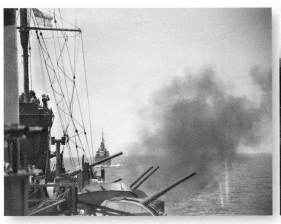

El Atiqa; the 2/14th Battalion some 2 miles further inland would prevent the movement of Vichy troops along the Beit ed Dine road; and the 2/27th Battalion would push north from El Haram, clear the northern bank of the Damour River of enemy troops and push through to El Boum, Er Roumane, and finally Daraya. The two battalions of the 17th Brigade (the 2/3rd and 2/5th) would then pass through the lines and cut any possible Vichy retreat along the road leading north from Damour. The 25th Brigade played its part in the battle by operating further inland in the Jezzine–Beit ed Dine area.

The operation was given essential support by accurate and heavy fire from HM Ships *Naiad*, *Ajax*, *Jackal*, *Kimberley*, *Havock* and *Hasty* and HMA Ships *Nizam* and *Perth*, which had spent the weeks preceding the battle battering Vichy artillery and infantry positions over a wide stretch of the coast. The fire was so heavy, accurate and relentless that Henri de Wailly's history of the campaign described victory in the Battle of Damour as being 'snatched by the sailors'.

The battle was also supported by the largest concentration of artillery mustered by Australian forces in World War II. Brigadier Berryman, returned to his role as 7th Division artillery commander after the dissolution of Berryforce, had at his disposal the 2/4th, 2/5th and 2/6th Field regiments (25-pdrs), two troops from the 2/9th Field Regiment (4.5in. howitzers) and 212th Medium Battery, Royal Artillery (6in. howitzers): 62 guns, carefully placed in the rugged terrain with vast amounts of ammunition. The six-hour-long bombardment began shortly after midnight on 6 July.

In the skies above the battle, No. 3 Squadron RAAF (Tomahawks) and No. 45 Squadron RAF (Blenheims) operated under command of the 7th Division from their respective bases at Rosh Pinna and Muquibila. The fighter squadron was unable to offer much by way of strafing Vichy troops, owing to good Vichy air cover and a tendency to move troops at night, but the Blenheims (escorted by the Tomahawks) performed more than 50 bombing sorties over Vichy positions throughout the battle. On 10 July three Blenheims on a bombing raid to Hammara were lost when attacked by Dewoitine fighters.

The main attack began on the morning of 6 July when the 2/27th Battalion clambered through the steep-sided Damour River valley near El Labiye and set about establishing a bridgehead by making for the high country near El Boum. Finding it deserted, the battalion pressed on against pockets of Vichy defenders in the rugged country, and by the end of the day was occupying the ridge around Daraya.

The Battle of Damour, 6–9 July 1941

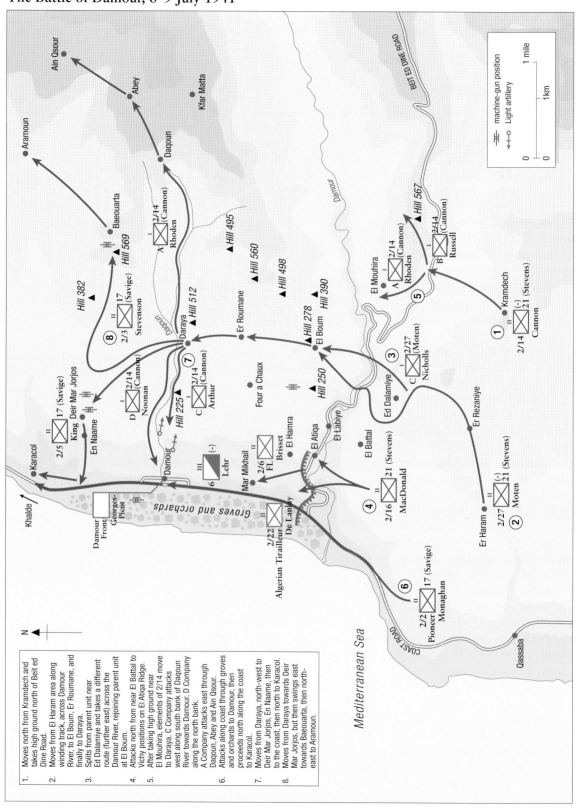

1. Moves north from Kramdech and takes high ground north of Beit ed Dine Road.
2. Moves from El Haram area along winding track, across Damour River, to El Boum, Er Roumane, and finally to Daraya.
3. Splits from parent unit near Ed Dalamiye and takes a different route (further east) across the Damour River, rejoining parent unit at El Boum.
4. Attacks north from near El Battal to Vichy positions on El Atiqa Ridge.
5. After taking high ground near El Mouhira, elements of 2/14 move to Daraya. C Company attacks west along south bank of Daqoun River towards Damour, D Company along the north bank.
   A Company attacks east through Daqoun, Abey and Ain Qsour.
6. Attacks along coast through groves and orchards to Damour, then proceeds north along the coast to Karacol.
7. Moves from Daraya, north-west to Deir Mar Jorjos, En Naame, then to the coast, then north to Karacol.
8. Moves from Daraya towards Deir Mar Jorjos, but then swings east towards Baeouarta, then north-east to Aramoun.

86

Further east, the 2/14th Battalion advanced to take control of the east–west road leading to Beit ed Dine, along which the Vichy could launch a powerful counter-attack into the Allied flank. After clambering over the steep and rocky tracks that characterized the battle inland, it established a roadblock and took the high ground overlooking the road at El Mouhira. Throughout the day the battalion saw off seven determined Vichy counter-attacks, and held firm. The high ground proved to be of tremendous importance for the Allied attack. From El Mouhira, troops of the 2/14th Battalion had views over the Beit ed Dine road and the country over which the 2/27th was attacking.

Blenheims of No. 45 Squadron RAF score a direct hit on Dentz's residence in Beirut, the Résidence des Pins, 30 June 1941. The attack was successful in destroying its target, but Dentz was not at home at the time. (Australian War Memorial, P02018.419)

The heaviest fighting fell to the depleted 2/16th Battalion, charged with attacking the El Atiqa Ridge close to the coast. The ridge and surrounding hills were the strongpoints of Vichy defences in the area; not expecting the Allies to be able to make a serious attack across the steep Damour Valley further inland, Vichy commanders had concentrated their efforts on the coast. The 2/16th Battalion climbed barbed-wired and orchard-covered terraces under a shower of mortar fire, enfilading machine-gun fire and grenades rolled down the steep slope. Despite heavy resistance the men pushed forward, and by the morning of 7 July were consolidating their position along the El Atiqa Ridge and surrounding high ground in preparation for a Vichy counter-attack.

The 2/16th Battalion's actions in the first days of the Battle of Damour were remarkable. Having attacked the strongest section of the Vichy defences, they succeeded against all odds. Allen and Stevens had not expected them to succeed. Their attack was hoped, at best, to tie up Vichy defenders from countering the attacks further east. While the French later estimated that they had been attacked by a force of at least four battalions at El Atiqa, the 2/16th Battalion at the start of the attack had numbered just 263 men.

On 7 July two companies of the 2/14th Battalion pressed north, passed through the 2/27th Battalion lines at Daraya and headed due west along the Daqoun River towards Damour. After encountering enemy patrols and machine-gun nests along the Daqoun River valley, C Company captured six machine guns, 10,000 rounds of ammunition and 300 grenades in the hills south of the Daqoun River; D Company entered the outskirts of Damour and occupied stone buildings which provided protection from Vichy counter-attacks and artillery, as well as from friendly fire from Allied ships that did not know their position in town. Both units captured dozens of Senegalese prisoners.

By gaining a foothold on the El Atiqa ridge, taking the high ground east of Damour and blocking the road to Beit ed Dine, the three battalions of the 21st Brigade had set the stage for the second phase of the battle in which the 17th Brigade would pass through their lines and continue to surround the defending Vichy French. This movement began on the night of 6/7 July. The 2/3rd and 2/5th battalions began moving north from the El Haram area and in the darkness pushed single file along the difficult inland

Members of the 2/16th Battalion after the heavy fighting at Damour. (Australian War Memorial, 008603)

tracks. The tracks were too steep for pack mules, so the men each carried 48 hours' rations, more than 50 rounds of ammunition (some as much as 300), two grenades, one sticky bomb, a blanket and a full water bottle. Many found it easiest to slide down the steep slopes on their backsides.

Despite heavy Vichy artillery and machine-gun fire from surrounding ridges, the 2/3rd Battalion managed to reach the high ground near the village of Deir Mar Jorjos on 8 July. As was so often the case in the campaign, the exhausted men were required to climb and take the peaks of the steep ridges so as to prevent enemy artillery and machine-gun fire from commanding the surrounding countryside. After a sharp fight against well-defended Vichy positions, the 2/3rd Battalion took command of the high country by the afternoon of 9 July, assisting the slow encirclement of the French at Damour.

Elements of the 2/5th Battalion clambered over the rugged country, passed through Deir Mar Jorjos and climbed down from the mountains to the coast, where it formed a roadblock on the main road leading north out of town. A battalion of the *29e Régiment de Tirailleurs Algériens*, hastily brought from the Damascus sector, was observed preparing for a counter-attack against the weak and exhausted Australian position, but an artillery observer from the 2/5th Field Regiment at Deir Mar Jorjos calling in heavy fire from his own unit and a troop of the 7th Medium Regiment, Royal Artillery broke the Vichy attack before it began. The encirclement of Damour was complete.

The bridge over the Damour was destroyed by Vichy forces while preparing defences. It was not fixed until 7 July, after which point cavalry could finally be brought into the fight on the Allied side. (Public Domain)

Having spent the previous day making a series of costly and failed attacks through the banana plantations abutting the Mediterranean Sea, troops of the 2/2nd Pioneer Battalion and 6th Australian Division Cavalry entered Damour on 9 July. They found the town abandoned, the Vichy defenders having escaped north on the night of 8/9 July.

On 9 July the Australian units who had attacked Damour began to meet up in the town. Damour was theirs, but the advance was not over. Almost as soon as the town was taken, the Australians continued to push north and consolidate their positions in the area, taking a wireless tower at Khalde, a roadblock well defended by Algerian troops and the high ground to the east near Abey and Aramoun.

Allied troops were in these positions south of Beirut on the night of 11/12 July, when the campaign came to an end.

THE WAR AT SEA

Allied naval activities ensured that the Vichy French were unable to bring in supplies of men and materiel. This strangulation of the Vichy war effort played a large part in their capitulation. On 25 June the Allies increased their significant advantages at sea when the submarine HMS *Parthian* sunk the Requin-class Vichy submarine *Souffleur*. Days later the Vichy government was able to persuade the German Armistice Commission to allow them to send troops to the campaign in Syria and Lebanon. Unable to get the troops safely to the region by land or air, the Vichy French were forced to risk bringing in reinforcements by sea in two transports, *Saint-Didier* and *Oued-Yquem*, escorted as much as possible by destroyers from Beirut and *Aéronavale* aircraft. *Saint-Didier* made it as far as the Gulf of Adalia off Turkey before it was sunk on 4 July by an Albacore of 829 Squadron, Fleet Air Arm, with the loss of 52 lives. In subsequent days *Oued-Yquem* sailed for an Italian base on Rhodes – reinforcement of the Levant was impossible.

AFTERMATH

The breach of defences at Damour was the end of Vichy ambitions to hold out in Syria and Lebanon. The Australians were pushing north only miles from Beirut; the British held the entrance to the Bekaa Valley at Merdjayoun; Free French and British forces were heading towards Aleppo; and Indian forces were taking command of northern Syria from Iraq. On 8 July Dentz ordered remaining Vichy ships and aircraft to leave the region so as to be able to fight another day (taking more than 50 Australian and British prisoners) and approached the American Consul General in Beirut, Cornelius van Engert, to sue for peace. A ceasefire came into effect at one minute past midnight on 12 July (though some shelling continued to occur across the front), and Wilson and de Verdilhac signed the document that brought the campaign to an end – the Armistice of Saint Jean d'Acre – two days later.

As the British wanted to strike a conciliatory tone (and possibly woo some French to the Allied side), the French were afforded full military honours, officers and other ranks were allowed to keep their individual weapons (though not ammunition) and French civil and military personnel were given the option of rallying to the Allied cause. Only around 5,500 of the nearly 40,000 of those given the option chose to join the Free French.

An epilogue for the campaign came when it was discovered that a number of Allied prisoners of war, who were guaranteed release by the terms of the Armistice, were being held by Dentz possibly as a bargaining chip. The prisoners, all officers, had been taken to Athens and moved to

BELOW LEFT
General Wilson initialling the Armistice, 12 July 1941. (Keystone-France/Gamma-Rapho via Getty Images)

BELOW RIGHT
Australian and Vichy French troops exchange cigarettes in Beirut, 15 July 1941. (Australian War Memorial, 021274)

France, rather than returned to British authorities. The issue was resolved on 31 July by a British ultimatum: if the prisoners were not returned within two days, the same number of Vichy officers, including Dentz and Jeannekyn (commander of the air force), would be arrested. The Allied prisoners were swiftly released.

The Syria–Lebanon campaign occupies an unusual place in the history of World War II. The confusing nature of its causes and the ambiguous nature of the enemy has seen the campaign left in the too-hard basket of popular memory. Overshadowed by events preceding it in Greece and continuing battles in North Africa, when Hitler invaded the Soviet Union on

Members of the I Australian Corps Ski School in Lebanon, 1941. Allied troops remained stationed in Syria and Lebanon for the rest of the war. Lebanon gained independence in 1943, Syria in 1946. (Photo: G. R. Frankland, Australian War Memorial, 022338)

The Last Post at Hammana, east of Beirut, October 1941. (Photo: Frank Hurley, Australian War Memorial, 010451)

22 June 1941, attention shifted to this new front. The British press tended to downplay the extent of Vichy French defence against the British attack, perhaps to ensure that public perceptions of France as Britain's friend and ally remained at the forefront of public imagination.

Veterans of the campaign and historians have questioned whether the campaign was necessary. In 1941 many British and Australian soldiers came to resent the Free French for drawing them into what they saw as a de Gaullist boondoggle and unnecessary waste of life. They felt Churchill had been duped into agreeing to the campaign under the false belief that it would be a brief and easy fight that would bring vast new numbers of troops to the Free French cause; to rub salt into the wounds, British, Australians and Indians had been left to do the majority of fighting.

De Gaulle's ambitions were, of course, not the only reason for the British to invade Syria and Lebanon. Britain had long feared that Nazi Germany would use Vichy territories in the Middle East as a base for operations, and Germany's use of Syrian air bases confirmed fears that increasing German influence in the area could deal the Allies a decisive strategic blow. While it is now known that Germany had no intentions of landing an army in Syria or Lebanon – being too busy planning to invade the Soviet Union – given Germany's ascendancy in the war up to that point, including recent victories in Greece and Crete, it is fair to conclude that those making the decision to proceed with Operation *Exporter* were justified: the Syria–Lebanon campaign neutralized a potential strategic threat at a time when strategic threats were thick on the ground.

No reliable figures exist for exact losses in the Syria–Lebanon campaign; the most commonly cited tally sits at about 2,400 dead. The largest losses fell on the Vichy French, with roughly 1,100 – mostly colonial – troops killed. Among the Allies, 416 Australian deaths are recorded on the Australian War Memorial's Roll of Honour, British and Indian losses are rounded to about 600 and the Free French to 300. For these reasons alone, this campaign deserves better recognition.

BIBLIOGRAPHY

1941 Diary of Lieut. General Sir John Lavarack – transcribed from his hand-written entries by his son James W. Lavarack – Version 2001/10/01

Aitken, Edward, *The Story of the 2/2nd Pioneer Battalion* (Melbourne, 1953)

Australian unit diaries (AWM 52), available at http://www.awm.gov.au

Bellair, John, *From Snow to Jungle: A History of the 2/3rd Machine-Gun Battalion* (Sydney, 1987)

Bou-Nacklie, N.E., 'The Invasion of Syria and Lebanon: The Role of the Local Paramilitary', *Middle Eastern Studies*, vol. 30, pp. 512–29 (1994)

Burns, John, *The Brown and Blue Diamond at War: The Story of the 2/27th Battalion A.I.F.* (Adelaide, 1960)

Carver, Michael, *Second to None: The Royal Scots Greys – 1919–1945* (Glasgow, 1954)

Churchill, Winston, *The Second World War*, Vol. III: *The Grand Alliance* (London, 1950)

Clift, Ken, *War Dance: A Story of the 2/3 Aust. Inf. Battalion A.I.F.* (Kingsgrove, NSW, 1980)

Crooks, William, *The Footsoldiers: The Story of the 2/33rd Australian Infantry Battalion, A.I.F. in the War of 1939–45* (Australia, 1971)

de Wailly, Henri, *Invasion Syria 1941: Churchill and de Gaulle's Forgotten War* (London, 2016)

Dean, Peter, *The Architect of Victory: The Military Careers of Lieutenant-General Sir Frank Horton Berryman* (Victoria, 2011)

Gill, Hermon, *Australia in the War of 1939–1945: Royal Australian Navy, 1939–1942* (Canberra, 1957)

Herington, John, *Australia in the War of 1939–1945: Air War against Germany and Italy, 1939–1943* (Canberra, 1954)

Ibrahim, Mahommed, *History of the First Punjab Regiment: 1759–1956* (Aldershot, 1958)

James, Richard, *Australia's War with France: The Campaign in Syria and Lebanon, 1941* (NSW, 2017)

Joslen, H.F., *Orders of Battle: United Kingdom and Colonial Formations and Units in the Second World War 1939–1945* (London, 1960)

Kemp, P.K., *The Staffordshire Yeomanry (Q.O.R.R.) in the First and Second World Wars 1914–1918 and 1939–1945* (Aldershot, 1950)

Laffin, John, *Forever Forward: The Story of the 2/31st Infantry Battalion, 2nd AIF, 1940–45* (NSW, 1994)

Long, Gavin, *Australia in the War of 1939–1945: Greece, Crete and Syria* (Canberra, 1953)

Martin, T.A., *The Essex Regiment: 1929–1950* (Essex, 1952)

McAlester, Jim, and Trigellis-Smith, Syd, *Largely a Gamble: Australians in Syria, June–July 1941* (Sydney, 1995)

Mockler, Anthony, *Our Enemies the French: Being an Account of the War Fought between the French & the British – Syria 1941* (London, 1976)

O'Brien, John, *Guns and Gunners: The Story of the 2/5th Australian Field Regiment in World War II* (Sydney, 1950)

Pal, Dharm, *Official History of the Indian Armed Forces in the Second World War 1939–1945: Campaign in Western Asia* (Calcutta, 1957)

Parkinson, Cyril, *Always a Fusilier: The War History of the Royal Fusiliers (City of London Regiment) 1939–1945* (London, 1949)

Platt, John, *The Royal Wiltshire Yeomanry (Prince of Wales' Own), 1907–1967* (London, 1972)

Playfair, I.S.O., *The Mediterranean and Middle East*, Vol. II: *The Germans Come to the Help of their Ally (1941)* (London, 1956)

Richards, Denis, *Royal Air Force 1939–1945*, Vol. I: *The Fight at Odds* (London, 1953)

Russell, William, *The Second Fourteenth Battalion: A History of an Australian Infantry Battalion in the Second World War* (Sydney, 1948)

Seaton, Daniel, 'Fighting against the French: Australians in the Allied invasion of Lebanon and Syria, 1941', *Australian War Memorial Summer Scholars Research Paper*, pp. 1–19 (2019)

Shores, Christopher, *Dust Clouds in the Middle East: The Air War for East Africa, Iraq, Syria, Iran and Madagascar, 1940–42* (London, 1996)

Smith, Colin, *England's Last War against France: Fighting Vichy 1940–1942* (Great Britain, 2009)

Trigellis-Smith, Syd, *All the King's Enemies: A History of the 2/5th Australian Infantry Battalion* (Australia, 1988)

Uren, Malcolm, *A Thousand Men at War: The Story of the 2/16th Battalion. A.I.F.* (Loftus, 2009 [1959])

Woodward, Sir Llewellyn, *British Foreign Policy in the Second World War*, Vol. I (London, 1970)

The Commonwealth War Cemetery in Damascus, 1943. The cemetery now contains 1,165 Commonwealth burials and commemorations from the two World Wars. (State Library of Victoria, H99.206/2926)

INDEX

Figures in **bold** refer to illustrations.